W9-BYF-708

The Lord Chamberlain is commanded by
The Queen to invite

....

....

to the Marriage of
His Royal Highness Prince William of Wales, K.G.
with
Miss Catherine Middleton
at Westminster Abbey
on Friday, 29th April, 2011 at 11.00 a.m.

A reply is requested to:
State Invitations Secretary, Lord Chamberlain's Office,
Buckingham Palace, London SW1A 1AA

Dress: Uniform, Morning Coat
or Lounge Suit

STERLING
New York

An Imprint of Sterling Publishing
387 Park Avenue South
New York, NY 10016

ISBN 978-1-4027-8816-1

Distributed in Canada by Sterling Publishing c/o Canadian Manda Group,
165 Dufferin Street, Toronto, Ontario, Canada M6K 3H6
Distributed in the United Kingdom by GMC Distribution Services
Castle Place, 166 High Street, Lewes, East Sussex, England BN7 1XU
Distributed in Australia by Capricorn Link (Australia) Pty. Ltd.
P.O. Box 704, Windsor, NSW 2756, Australia

Please see page 222 through 224 for text and picture credits

For information about custom editions, special sales, and premium and corporate purchases, please contact Sterling Special Sales at 800-805-5489 or specialsales@sterlingpublishing.com.

Manufactured in Canada

2 4 6 8 10 9 7 5 3 1

www.sterlingpublishing.com

William & Catherine

Their Romance and Royal Wedding in Photographs

Including a Brief Photographic History of British Royal Weddings

Created by David Elliot Cohen

Foreword by Robert Jobson

News of the World Royal Editor and
NBC Royal Commentator

STERLING

New York

God our Father, we thank you for our families; for the love that we share; and for the joy of our marriage.

—PRAYER WRITTEN BY THE BRIDE AND GROOM AND DELIVERED AT THEIR WEDDING BY THE RIGHT REVEREND RICHARD CHARTRES, BISHOP OF LONDON

MOMENTOUS OCCASION: Right, the newly married Duke and Duchess of Cambridge and their nineteen hundred wedding guests listen to the bishop of London deliver his address following the exchange of vows at Westminster Abbey. **Preceding pages**, after the royal wedding, carriages bearing William and Catherine and the queen and Prince Philip, respectively, are escorted by divisions of the Captain's Escort and the Sovereign's Escort up the festooned Mall toward Buckingham Palace.

Photographs by Chris Ison (preceding pages) and Dominic Lipinski (right)

EVERYONE'S WEDDING

By Robert Jobson

News of the World Royal Editor,
NBC Royal Commentator, and Royal Author

Their wedding day was the crowning moment of the first grand act in the theater of royalty in this century. It was pomp and pageantry at its finest, a resplendent symbol of British national pride and unity played out on the perfect stage: Westminster Abbey—the setting for a thousand years of royal history.

Perhaps one moment more than any other showed what the monarchy has become and possibly what it will be. "Are you ready?" asked Prince William. "Okay, let's …"

The prince leaned toward his beautiful bride, Catherine Elizabeth Middleton—the newly ennobled Her Royal Highness the Duchess of Cambridge. They kissed not once but twice, to the delight of the million-strong crowd tightly packed along the Mall opposite Buckingham Palace. Moments later, World War II fighter planes roared overhead in the flypast. It was all timed to military precision. The Buckingham Palace publicity machine could not have asked for anything better for the royal couple's first public appearance as husband and wife.

But this was not a kiss just for the cameras; this was the real thing, and everyone watching, including the estimated two billion glued to their televisions around the world,

LIKE A MELODY: As she walked from her Rolls-Royce Phantom VI toward Westminster Abbey, Catherine Middleton revealed one of the best-kept secrets of modern times—her bridal gown. Designed by Sarah Burton, creative director of the British fashion house Alexander McQueen, the well-reviewed dress—Hamish Bowles of *Vogue* called it "sublime"—was reminiscent of Grace Kelly's 1956 wedding gown.

Photograph by Ian Langsdon

knew it. Personally, I felt emotional—proud and emotional. Only the most cynical among us wouldn't. My ringside seat to history—commentating for a leading US network, NBC—gave me a perfect viewpoint from the specially erected television studios at Canada Gate opposite the palace. The kiss was a wonderful touch, an iconic moment in the history of this new, modern monarchy.

Earlier, with two words, "I will"—so softly spoken—Catherine sent cheers ringing around the country and the far-flung parts of the world that still hold monarchy at its heart. And with that, the onetime commoner Catherine, in an instant, took the giant step into the magical world of royalty, destined now to be the future queen consort of sixteen nations across the globe.

Together, William and Catherine erased the sadness of our recent royal past and evoked memories of happier times, when we still believed in fairy-tale royal marriages that would last. It was the most anticipated and watched event in Britain's long history—perhaps in world history, given the immediate global reach of today's media—eclipsing even the terrible sadness of Princess Diana's funeral played out on the same stage of the Abbey. Catherine's words of commitment restored our faith. At last, the monarchy could move on, and Diana, an icon of the last century, could rest in peace.

This was, quite simply, a very good day for royalists. And for the House of Windsor, created by George V out of necessity nearly a century earlier, it was simply sensational. Catherine was the perfect new recruit to their clan. The descendant of working miners, she oozed class and natural grace. She had—like a previous princess, her new husband's late mother—a natural nobility about her. Both Catherine and Diana were utterly unflappable as they delivered their vows. And as he placed the band of Welsh gold, William steadied himself for the next chapter in this long royal story. The queen concurred. "It was amazing," she said.

But what I liked were the lighter, more personal touches: "Are you happy?" Catherine asked her husband as she climbed into the 1902 open State Landau. "It was amazing, amazing," replied the duke. "I am so proud you're my wife." The most striking aspect of the whole occasion was the simplest of the lot: two people so at one with each other.

Tradition dictates that royal men and their new wives receive a title on their wedding day—and often more than one. As well as a duchess, Miss Middleton is now technically Princess William of Wales. According to protocol, she is not officially Princess Catherine, as she was not born a princess in her own right. Instead she adopts her husband's first name.

But for William, a man with his finger on the pulse of his people, it is not about titles. This, for him, was their day, and he was determined to keep it that way. At this moment this young couple, the royal faces of the Facebook generation, became the most famous people on the planet.

When William first set eyes on Kate at the University of St. Andrews in September 2001, he said he instantly knew there was something special about her. They became friends first. They shared the same major, history of art, before William switched to geography, and they lived in the same residence hall, known as Sallies.

Catherine was once asked if she felt fortunate to date Prince William. Quick as a flash she replied with supreme self-confidence: "He's lucky to be going out with me." She ticked all the right boxes for a future queen consort, but was no fawning subject desperate to marry into royalty. Theirs is a true love match.

The day after the wedding — the pomp and pageantry over — the newlyweds dressed casually before flying off in a helicopter on the shortest of breaks. Their honeymoon was put on hold as William was compelled to return to RAF duties as a search and rescue pilot just a few days later.

The couple sent a message to the nation, thanking all for their support on the "most wonderful day of our lives," and the new Duchess of Cambridge said of their glittering wedding: "I'm glad the weather held off. We had a great day."

But just twenty-four hours later, the newly ennobled Duke and Duchess of Cambridge were Mr. and Mrs. Ordinary again. The pair — who often used the pseudonym Mr. and Mrs. Smith whenever they checked into a hotel as students — looked just like any other young couple going on a weekend away. On the day, perhaps overwhelmed by the splendor and formality of the wedding, they seemed to forget to hold hands. But twenty-four hours later they walked hand in hand, smiling, before boarding the helicopter. In an instant they were gone, but the whirlwind of goodwill they had created was not forgotten.

Walter Bagehot, the brilliant Victorian journalist and constitutional expert, was right all those years ago: a princely marriage really does rivet mankind.

For this was our wedding too, and we were all happy to be a part of it.

THE WEDDING OF QUEEN VICTORIA AND PRINCE ALBERT OF SAXE-COBURG AND GOTHA, 1840: A contemporaneous illustration of Queen Victoria, Britain's longest-reigning monarch, on her wedding day, February 10, 1840. At twenty-one, Queen Victoria married her first cousin, Prince Albert of Saxe-Coburg and Gotha. "The queen, as brides generally do, looked pale and anxious," recalled nineteenth-century biographer James Parton. "Her dress was a rich white satin, trimmed with orange blossoms, and upon her head she wore a wreath of the same beautiful flowers."

Victoria's groom, Prince Albert, was initially unpopular with her subjects, who considered him a minor royal from an impoverished German state. But the prince consort eventually gained favor as Victoria's closest advisor, best friend, and father of their nine children. When forty-two-year-old Albert died in 1861, probably of typhoid fever, Victoria sank into a deep depression. For the next seven years, the queen rarely appeared in public. She wore only black mourning clothes until her death in 1901. Victoria was buried beside her husband in a mausoleum she built for the purpose. Her words, inscribed above the door, read: "Farewell best beloved, here at last I shall rest with thee…."

GRAND AFFAIRS

A Brief History of British Royal Weddings

As the role of the British royal family has evolved from a more political to a more symbolic capacity, royal weddings have followed suit. When British monarchs possessed consequential political and military power — prior to the late nineteenth century — royal weddings were relatively simple affairs that marked the consummation of a political alliance.

In 1625, when King Charles I rejected a union with the infanta of Spain in favor of Princess Henrietta Maria of France, the implications were clear: Charles would not convert to Catholicism as the Spanish king demanded, and the Kingdom of England, Scotland, and Ireland would pursue a pro-French, rather than a pro-Spanish, foreign policy. Charles, who was married by proxy, didn't even bother to show up at his lavish Paris wedding.

Despite their private nature, some pre-twentieth century British royal weddings initiated customs to which we still adhere. Sixteenth-century King Henry VIII was a remarkably bad husband, but his original marriage vows, "to have and to hold from this day forward, for better or worse, for richer and poorer, in sickness and in health, 'til death do us part," still bind couples throughout the English-speaking world every weekend. Queen Victoria is widely credited with popularizing the elaborate white wedding gown; prior to her 1840 marriage, brides wore colorful dresses that could be worn again.

As Britain's constitutional monarchy became more constitutional and less monarchical, royal weddings evolved into public spectacles designed to bind British subjects to their royal family. The future George V's 1893 wedding to Princess Mary of Teck was a triumphant extravaganza that featured ten royal princesses as bridesmaids and the crowned heads of Europe as witnesses. The crowds, as they say, went wild. The 1922 wedding of their daughter, Princess Alice, filled the streets of London, and the nuptials of their granddaughter, the future Elizabeth, raised the spectacle to a new level.

But it was not until the age of television that the vast drawing power of royal weddings emerged. First came the 1960 wedding of Queen Elizabeth's younger sister, Princess Margaret, to Antony Armstrong-Jones. The marriage would be a disaster, but more than 20 million people watched the magnificent ceremony. The worldwide audience spiked to 100 million — nearly twice the population of Britain — when Queen Elizabeth's only daughter, Princess Anne, married Mark Phillips in 1973. It reached 750 million, or a sixth of the world's population, for 1981's "wedding of the century," when Prince Charles married Lady Diana, and well exceeded a billion souls when Prince William married Catherine. As a point of comparison, only half a billion people watched the first human land on the moon.

So what is it about a British royal wedding that attracts spectators of every race, creed, and nationality? Why do these ceremonies bind us together as one worldwide congregation? Certainly, as human beings, we all love ritual. And no one does ritual better than the British royal family, and never so well as at a royal wedding. But more essentially, we all love love, and British royal weddings may be love's grandest, most elaborate expression.

ALBERT EDWARD, PRINCE OF WALES, AND PRINCESS ALEXANDRA OF DENMARK, 1863: When Victoria and Albert sought a wife for their eldest son, Albert Edward (later, King Edward VII) they enlisted the aid of his older sister, Crown Princess Victoria of Prussia. Victoria eventually settled upon Alexandra, the charming sixteen-year-old daughter of Prince Christian IX, a previously minor royal who clinched Denmark's throne in a succession dispute.

Politically, the choice was surprising: Victoria's Prussia and Christian's Denmark would soon clash over the disputed duchy of Schleswig. But as queen, the dignified, affable Alexandra was a great success. Immensely popular with her British subjects, Alexandra bore five living children, became an early fashion icon and gracefully tolerated her debonair husband's many mistresses (including the great-grandmother of Prince Charles's longtime mistress, now wife, Camilla Parker-Bowles.)

Although they were well loved throughout their reign, Edward and Alexandra's wedding disappointed the British public and press. Windsor Castle was inaccessible to London's adoring crowds, and the court, still in mourning for Prince Albert, allowed female guests to wear only muted shades of gray, lilac, and mauve.

I could have been quite happy and contented living in a cottage, if I had been able to share my intellectual interests and intellectual aspirations with a husband whose strong, protective love would have guided me around the rocks.

—PRINCESS ALICE, IN A LETTER TO HER HUSBAND TWO YEARS BEFORE HER DEATH

PRINCESS ALICE AND DUKE LOUIS IV OF HESSE AND BY RHINE, 1862: In a makeshift studio at Osborne House, on the windblown Isle of Wight, Princess Alice's wedding party includes, **l–r,** the bride's younger brother, Prince Arthur; the bridegroom and the bride's older brother, Prince Albert Edward of Wales.

Queen Victoria's kind, devoted, and sensitive third child married her minor, not-very-wealthy German prince, for love not money, but few modern royal weddings have been as dismal. The weather was cold and gloomy; only relatives were invited; and the queen and her son, Alfred—still mourning Victoria's recently deceased husband—wept throughout the ceremony. Victoria would later tell her poet laureate, Alfred, Lord Tennyson, that it was "the saddest day I can remember," and write to her eldest daughter, Victoria, that "it was more of a funeral than a wedding."

The bride and groom soon discovered that they had little in common. The princess, whose intellectual and socially conscious pursuits were well ahead of her time, died along with her youngest daughter during a diphtheria epidemic when Alice was thirty-five. Her sixth child, Alexandra, née Alix of Hesse, would later marry Tsar Nicholas II of Russia, and their entire family would be executed during the Russian Revolution.

*There's only one
thing I never did
and wish I had done:
climbed over a fence.*

— QUEEN MARY OF TECK

PRINCE GEORGE, DUKE OF YORK, AND PRINCESS MARY OF TECK, 1893: The wedding of the future George V and his bride, a twenty-six-year-old princess from an impecunious German-English family, was a spectacular affair at London's St. James's Palace. Crowds gathered; ten princesses served as bridesmaids; and rulers of Russia, Denmark, Belgium, and Prussia attended the festivities.

While their wedding—and marriage—were both triumphant, George and Mary's road to the altar was rocky. The groom originally fell in love with his cousin, Marie of Edinburgh, who refused his proposal for political reasons and instead married the future king of Romania. The bride was first engaged to George's older brother, Albert Victor, but Albert died of influenza six weeks after proposing. Upon his death, George became heir apparent, and his grandmother, Queen Victoria, continued to champion Princess Mary as the best wife for a future king. George proposed to Mary in May 1893, after which they fell deeply in love. For the rest of their lives, George wrote to Mary every day they were apart; and unlike his famously promiscuous father, Edward VII, George never took a mistress.

Photograph by W. and D. Downey

THE ROYAL WEDDING.

PHOTO,
VANDYK, Ltd.
LADY D. GORDON-LENNOX. LADY E. BOWES-LYON.
LADY MARY CAMBRIDGE. PRINCESS MAUD.

VISCOUNT PRINCESS
LASCELLES. MARY.   MAJOR SIR VICTOR MACKENZIE.   LADY D. BRIDGEMAN.
LADY RACHEL CAVENDISH.   LADY MARY THYNNE.

532.W.
BEAGLES' POSTCARDS
LADY MAY CAMBRIDGE.

PRINCESS MARY AND HENRY, VISCOUNT LASCELLES, 1922: This postcard commemorates the wedding of King George and Queen Mary's only daughter, Mary Victoria Alexandra Alice—Alice to the family—and the immensely wealthy future Earl of Harewood, fifteen years her senior.

The groom, who distinguished himself as an army officer during the Great War, was known at the time as "the richest soldier in the world." Lascelles, who stood to inherit one of England's grandest stately homes and 30,000 Yorkshire acres, had already received a £2.5 million bequest from his great uncle. (The modern equivalent would be $140 million.) Among the bridesmaids is, third from left, Lady Elizabeth Bowes-Lyon, a close friend of the bride, who would subsequently wed King George VI and give birth to Queen Elizabeth II.

PUBLIC HOLIDAY: A royal coach with outriders and three liveried footmen carries Princess Mary and Viscount Lascelles to their wedding at Westminster Abbey. The ceremony drew the largest crowds, to date, for a state event. Nine thousand police were deployed, and more than 500 spectators fainted in the crush. According to the Associated Press, "The West End resounded with song and merriment until nearly 3 o'clock [in the] morning in celebration of the wedding."

*We must take what is coming
and make the best of it.*

— PRINCESS ELIZABETH TO PRINCE ALBERT, UPON
LEARNING THAT THEY WOULD BECOME QUEEN AND KING

PRINCE ALBERT, DUKE OF YORK, AND LADY ELIZABETH BOWES-LYON, 1924: The wedding portrait includes, l–r, the bride's father, Claude George Bowes-Lyon, 14th Earl of Strathmore and Kinghorne; the bride's mother, Cecilia, Countess of Strathmore; the bride; the groom; the groom's mother, Queen Mary; and the groom's father, King George V.

When Elizabeth Bowes-Lyon, daughter of an unpretentious Scottish aristocrat and the ninth of ten children, finally married George V's second son, she could not imagine her future. Wary of royal life, she rejected Albert's proposal twice before acquiescing. Twelve years into their happy, quiet marriage, George's older brother, Edward VIII, abdicated the throne to marry Wallis Simpson, a divorced American socialite. A constitutional crisis ensued, and shy, stammering Albert (immortalized in the Oscar-winning film *The King's Speech*) succeeded his brother as George VI—a *nom de règne* chosen to emphasize continuity with his father. Elizabeth, the reluctant royal, was suddenly queen—a role she would play for fifteen years.

When her daughter, Elizabeth II, succeeded her father in 1952, Queen Elizabeth became the widowed queen mother for another half century. Although she was not always uniformly popular, Elizabeth's charm and grit eventually made her one of England's most genuinely loved women. King George won his nation's heart when he conquered his speech defect to rally Britain during World War II, but Elizabeth also inspired Britain during the war. When asked if she would remove her young daughters from London during the German Blitz, she famously replied, "The girls will not leave unless I do. I will not leave unless the king does. And the king will not leave under any circumstances whatsoever." Upon Elizabeth's death in 2002, at 101, she was eulogized as the mother, not only of a queen, but also of a nation.

I represented something that lay deep-rooted in their hearts: a loyal and loving respect for any member of their royal family.

— PRINCESS ALICE, DUCHESS OF GLOUCESTER, IN *MEMORIES OF NINETY YEARS*, 1991

PRINCE HENRY, DUKE OF GLOUCESTER, AND LADY ALICE MONTAGU-DOUGLAS-SCOTT, 1935: Greeting the crowd from the balcony of Buckingham Palace are, l–r, the nine-year-old future queen, Elizabeth; her grandfather, King George V, in the last year of his reign; five-year-old Princess Margaret; Princess Mary, Countess of Harewood; the groom; the bride; and the reigning British queen, Mary of Teck.

George V's third son, Prince Henry, age thirty-five, and his wealthy Scottish fiancée, Lady Alice Montagu-Douglas-Scott, age thirty-four, originally planned elaborate nuptials at Westminster Abbey. But when the bride's father died shortly before the wedding, the ceremony was moved to Buckingham Palace's private chapel.

The bride was well known as an adventurer who briefly lived in Kenya and famously smuggled herself into Afghanistan with army friends. Both she and her husband served in the military during World War II—Henry as second-in-command of the 20th Armoured Brigade, and Alice as head of the Women's Auxiliary Air Force. In 1944, the couple decamped to Australia, where Prince Henry served as governor-general for two years. Alice survived a serious auto accident in 1965 to become Britain's longest-lived royal. Born on Christmas Day 1901, she would die at age 102—nearly 103—beating her sister-in-law, the queen mother, by two years.

I think the main lesson we have learnt is that tolerance is the one essential ingredient in any happy marriage.... You can take it from me, the queen has the quality of tolerance in abundance.

— PRINCE PHILIP ON THE OCCASION OF HIS FIFTIETH
WEDDING ANNIVERSARY, 1997

PRINCESS ELIZABETH AND PHILIP, DUKE OF EDINBURGH, 1947: On November 20, 1947, the heiress to the British throne married a man she met when she was eight, loved when she was thirteen, and secretly agreed to marry when she was twenty. Philip, great-grandchild of Queen Victoria and a scion of Europe's aristocratic Battenberg family, was born a prince of both Greece and Denmark. But to marry his princess, he renounced both titles, joined the British Navy, and for eight months became plain old Lieutenant Philip Mountbatten (an English rendering of Battenberg). Princess Elizabeth's father, King George VI, restored Philip's HRH status the day before the wedding and created him Duke of Edinburgh the morning of the ceremony. But Philip wouldn't officially become a prince again—this time of Great Britain—until his wife, the queen, issued letters patent for her consort in 1957.

Princess Elizabeth's dress was designed by Sir Norman Hartnell and woven from silk produced by the Chinese silkworms at Lullingstone Castle, Kent. Her tulle veil was secured by a diamond tiara first given to Princess Mary of Teck by Queen Victoria in 1893, and then remade in 1919. Her wedding bouquet of white orchids, supplied by the Worshipful Company of Gardeners, includes a sprig of myrtle snipped from a bush grown from the original myrtle in Queen Victoria's wedding bouquet.

OFFICIAL CAKE: Mr. F. E. Schur, chief confectioner at McVitie & Price (established 1830) puts the final touches on the eight-foot-high official wedding cake of Princess Elizabeth and Philip, Duke of Edinburgh. (Eleven unofficial cakes were also received as gifts.) The cake features the armorial bearings of both families as well as regimental and naval badges. With postwar food rationing still in place in Britain, the Australian Girl Guides sent the ingredients for the official cake as a wedding present.

Photograph by J. A. Hampton

OFFICIAL PHOTO: After this photograph was snapped in the throne room at Buckingham Palace (on page 40, see an image of the newly married Prince Charles and Princess Diana posing in the same spot), the royal couple left for their wedding night at Broadlands, the Hampshire estate of Philip's uncle, Earl Mountbatten. They were joined on their honeymoon by Princess Elizabeth's corgi, Susan.

PRINCESS MARGARET AND ANTONY ARMSTRONG-JONES, FIRST EARL OF SNOWDON, 1960: The first televised British royal wedding was appropriately spectacular. Twenty million viewers watched Queen Elizabeth's younger sister, Princess Margaret, resplendent in white silk and a diamond tiara, alight from the Glass Coach outside Westminster Abbey. Accompanied by eight bridesmaids, Margaret and her brother-in-law, the Duke of Edinburgh, walked the abbey's blue-carpeted aisle to the altar, where she married her second choice: Antony Armstrong-Jones, the newly minted Earl of Snowdon. The princess had been dissuaded from marrying her first fiancé, a divorced commoner, by the Church of England and Britain's political establishment.

The charismatic Snowdon was a prominent photographer and a world-class philanderer. The marriage broke down, quickly and publicly, with cringe-worthy scandals on both sides. But it wasn't until 1978 that Margaret became the first royal to divorce since Henry VIII in 1533.

Above, Princess Margaret leaves Clarence House for her wedding at Westminster Abbey. **Left**, Princess Margaret and Antony Armstrong-Jones after the ceremony.

PRINCE CHARLES AND LADY DIANA SPENCER, 1981:
Lady Diana Spencer enters St. Paul's Cathedral trailing a twenty-five-foot train expertly managed by seventeen-year-old Lady Sarah Armstrong-Jones, the oldest of Diana's five bridesmaids. Diana's father, the 8th Earl Spencer, waves to the crowd.

By the time Prince Charles, the heir apparent, turned thirty-two, he was under distinct pressure to marry and father an heir. During his twenties and early thirties, Charles was linked to many young women. He even proposed to his second cousin, twenty-one-year-old Amanda Knatchbull, who allegedly replied, "What a funny idea." But more than a decade after the onset of the sexual revolution, few prospective brides could pass the unspoken "virginity test" for future queens. Charles's beloved uncle, Lord Mountbatten, advised the prince to "choose a suitable, attractive and sweet-charactered girl before she has met anyone else she might fall for." With that in mind, Charles proposed to the teenage daughter of an old aristocratic family (and the younger sister of a former girlfriend).

The fiancée of a British heir apparent has always been subject to public scrutiny, but in the age of global media, Lady Di became an instant worldwide celebrity. While twenty million people watched Princess Margaret wed in 1960, an estimated 750 million people, or 17 percent of the world's population at the time, watched Charles and Diana's fairy-tale wedding. Another 600,000 lined the parade route.

I desperately loved my husband and I wanted to share everything together, and I thought that we were a very good team.

— Princess Diana in a 1995 interview

BACKSTAGE: The new Princess of Wales comforts five-year-old Clementine Hambro, great-granddaughter of Winston Churchill and the youngest of her five bridesmaids. Also at Buckingham Palace are, **l–r**, bridesmaids India Hicks, age thirteen, and Sarah Jane Gaselee, age eleven, and, of course, Her Majesty, the Queen.

Photograph by Lichfield

SCENES FROM A FAIRY–TALE WEDDING: On July 29, 1981, a worldwide audience saw Prince Charles and Princess Diana, **left**, in the throne room of Buckingham Palace, **top**, riding from St. Paul's Cathedral to Buckingham Palace in an open landau and, **bottom**, kissing on the balcony of Buckingham Palace.

Photographs by Lichfield (left) and Reginald Davis (bottom)

GROWING UP ROYAL

The Less Than Private Life of Prince William

At seven pounds, one ounce, Baby Wales — his parents would not agree on William Arthur Philip Louis for several days — entered this world with a heavy load on his tiny shoulders. His arrival meant that the House of Windsor would likely retain the British monarchy well into the twenty-first century. At a more basic level, his advent burnished the odds that the monarchy itself would persist.

William's birth was particularly welcome because, at age thirty-three, Prince Charles had taken far longer than expected to perform his most basic function — begetting an heir. But beget he did — and with a beautiful, charismatic young princess from an older and arguably more aristocratic family than his own. (The Windsor line was founded in 1840; the Spencers have been noble since the fifteenth century.) It seemed in those early, halcyon days that Charles and Diana's "fairy-tale wedding" had segued nicely into a fairy-tale family.

The British people — at least the 75 percent of them who prefer a monarchy to a republic — celebrated William's arrival. Thousands gathered outside Buckingham Palace awaiting news of his delivery. Schools announced the happy event to their students; British Airways pilots notified their passengers; sports announcers interrupted World Cup coverage; and across the kingdom, entire pubs toasted the new heir apparent.

From the moment of his birth, William's life became a matter for public exposition and discussion. News photographers recorded his departure from St. Mary's Hospital.

AN HEIR IS BORN: A month before their first wedding anniversary, Diana and Charles emerge from St. Mary's Hospital Paddington with Prince William, the prospective king of England. The seven-pound infant, called "Baby Wales" for the first few days of his life, was born on the summer solstice, June 21, 1982, at 9:03 pm. Charles was ecstatic. In a break with royal tradition, and at Diana's request, he attended the difficult, sixteen-hour labor and birth. In a letter to a cousin he wrote, "I am so thankful I was beside Diana's bedside the whole time because I really felt as though I'd shared deeply in the process of birth and as a result was rewarded by seeing a small creature which belongs to us even though he seemed to belong to everyone else as well."

Reporters dutifully noted that he was the first British heir even to be born in a hospital, and that his father (at Diana's insistence) was the first Prince of Wales present at his own child's birth.

Fittingly, William took his first unassisted steps at a New Zealand press conference. His first day of nursery school, of elementary school, of boarding school, Eton and Saint Andrews were not just big events in the young prince's life. They were news stories and photo ops. Even as a child, his was a public life.

When William was ten years old his parents separated—traumatic for any child, but more so when the prime minister announces the event in the House of Commons. While Charles and Diana sniped at each other in the press, then bitterly divorced, every newspaper, magazine, and television and radio network in the English-speaking world and beyond incessantly covered the story—a fact that could hardly have gone unnoticed by young William. Even when his glamorous mother perished in a tragic auto accident, William was not afforded the luxury of private mourning. As princes of the realm, fifteen-year-old William and thirteen-year-old Harry were obliged, only days after Diana's death, to greet thousands of mourners gathered in front of Kensington Palace. The next day, they marched stone-faced down a crowd-lined avenue to their mother's funeral.

As William grew into a tall, handsome young man—at six foot three, the tallest prospective monarch in British history—he lived a life of privilege, shuttling between stately homes and castles, skiing in Switzerland, clubbing in London, polo at Cirencester, taking his pick of military assignments, and sponsoring glittering charity galas. But through it all, he needed always to remain mindful that his achievements and failures, romances, adventures, and indiscretions were observed, recorded, and publicly judged—the heavy burden of a future king.

BABY WILLS: It took a few days for the royal couple to choose a name. "We've thought of one or two," Charles told a reporter, "There's a bit of an argument about it, but we'll find one eventually." Charles wanted to call his son Arthur, but Diana preferred William, and she prevailed.

On August 4, 1982, in the Music Room at Buckingham Palace, the Right Reverend Robert Runcie, Archbishop of Canterbury, christened William Arthur Philip Louis. The infant's six godparents were all in attendance: Constantine II, King of the Hellenes; Norton Knatchbull, 8th Baron Brabourne; the South African writer Sir Laurens van der Post; HRH Princess Alexandra; Natalia Grosvenor, Duchess of Westminster; and Lady Susan Hussey, Woman of the Bedchamber to HM The Queen since 1960. **Right**, Mum, Dad, and baby "Wills" at Kensington Palace in 1982.

EARLY DAYS: The public nature of William's life was established early on. He was only nine months old when he first stood unassisted—at a packed press conference in New Zealand. Diana had flustered royal watchdogs when, against advice, she brought her cheerful, energetic young prince along for the six-week royal excursion through the antipodes. But, the new princess had a knack for public relations, and the goodwill-tour-with-diapers was a smash success, with observers comparing the adoring crowds to Beatlemania. A month later, the Waleses made a seventeen-day trip to Canada. This time, Wills stayed home, celebrating his first birthday with a nanny. Charles thought the boy was "too young to know the difference," but Diana felt "guilt—tons of it" for missing the event. **Above**, Charles, Diana, and baby Wills at Kensington Palace in 1983. **Right**, Wills and Diana pose for a portrait in 1984.

Photograph by Tim Graham (above)

STAGE PRESENCE: Above, the three-year-old prince is led inside for the annual Christmas play at Mrs. Mynors' nursery school in the Notting Hill section of London. Charles and Diana attended the ten-minute production, in which Wills played the part of a wolf. Prince William was the first royal heir to attend a regular nursery school alongside his future subjects.

Photograph by James Gray

HEIR SUPPORT: Like most two-year-olds, Wills became, in Diana's words, a "holy terror—dashing about, bumping into tables and lamps, breaking everything in sight." The "terrible twos" only got worse when brother Harry appeared in September 1984. But over time the princes formed a close bond, with the more circumspect Wills looking out for his free-spirited younger brother, and Harry making William's life a little more fun. **Left**, at home in Kensington Palace, October 1985, Wills helps one-year-old Harry with his first steps.

Photograph by Tim Graham

FLIGHT SCHOOL: Above, Wills, age four, checks out the controls of a Westland Wessex HCC Mk4, a helicopter in the Queen's Royal Flight. Snapped in 1986 at Highgrove, Prince Charles's Gloucestershire estate, this photo was released twenty-two years later when the prince began helicopter training for real—with the Royal Air Force Search and Rescue Force.

Photograph by Tim Graham

NET EFFECT: Right, dressed in a British Army Parachute Regiment uniform, Wills works off some energy on the play structure at Highgrove. Prince Charles, a former naval officer who qualified as both an RAF jet pilot and a Royal Navy helicopter pilot, hoped at least one of his sons would develop an interest in organic gardening, his passion at Highgrove's Duchy Home Farm. But, initially, William and Harry preferred higher adrenaline pursuits.

Photograph by Tim Graham

Luckily we've had the chance of growing up together, going through the same stuff as each other.... He is the one person on this earth, who I can actually really talk to about anything.

— PRINCE HARRY DISCUSSING HIS BROTHER, PRINCE WILLIAM, IN A 2005 INTERVIEW

WILD CHILD: Three-year-old Prince Harry lets his silly side fly on the Queen's official state birthday in June 1988. After the Trooping of the Color, a traditional military review at London's Horse Guards Parade, the royal family appeared on the balcony of Buckingham Palace, where they watched an RAF flyover. Sharing Harry's corner of the balcony are, **l–r**, his bemused older brother, Prince William, his not-so-amused mother, Princess Diana, and his cousins, The Ladies Gabriella and Rose Windsor.

Photograph by Tim Graham

ROYALS-IN-TRAINING: On June 29, 1989, four-year-old Harry and seven-year-old Wills strike their princely poses during Beating Retreat, a military ceremony performed annually for the royals. By this point, Wills knew that he would someday be king, but he didn't fully understand the limits of modern royal power. "He was always threatening to have us sent to the Tower," said one of his teachers, "either that or just executed by one of his bodyguards."

Photograph by Tim Graham

FIRST DAY OF SCHOOL: In September 1989, Headmistress Frederika Blair-Turner and old-timer Prince William welcome Harry, nearly five, to his first day at Wetherby, a West London school for four-to-eight-year-old boys. Princess Diana looks on. From nursery school to Wetherby, Ludgrove, and Eton, Harry would follow in his big brother's footsteps. They would part paths only when William opted for a university degree while Harry went directly to the military.

Photograph by Terry Fincher

SUNNY DAYS: Wills, Diana, and Harry on the chairlift in Lech—an Austrian ski resort colonized by the rich and famous in April 1991. Wills was on break from his first year at Ludgrove, a prominent all-boys boarding school in Berkshire, while Harry, age six, was still living at home. Their lives would soon change irrevocably.

Photograph by Tim Graham

WELCOME RELIEF: Charles and William at Klosters, the Prince of Wales's favored ski resort in February 1994, nearly three years after the photograph on the facing page was snapped. Much had transpired in the interim—most of it bad. In 1992, Charles's brother, Prince Andrew, separated from Sarah Ferguson; Princess Anne divorced Mark Phillips; and in June, royal watcher Andrew Morton sparked a media firestorm when he published *Diana: Her True Story*, a cri de coeur about the princess's loveless marriage. Six months later, Prime Minister John Major took the floor of the House of Commons to announce Charles and Diana's "amicable separation"—a somewhat disingenuous characterization considering the ongoing barrage of sniping and media leaks from both parties to the marriage.

Photograph by Tim Graham

He does so many amazing things. I only wish people would see that more.

— PRINCE WILLIAM SPEAKING ABOUT HIS FATHER IN A 2003 INTERVIEW

LIGHT MOMENT: Despite his parents' ongoing marital melodrama, played out incessantly in the press, William was maturing into a sensitive and accomplished young man. At Ludgrove School, he was captain of the rugby and hockey teams, head of the dramatic society, and in the top tier academically. A crack shot, William teamed up with his father to win a school skeet-shooting competition. Here, on August 19, 1995, Wills, age thirteen, and Charles attend the fiftieth anniversary of VJ Day, the end of World War II. Despite many press reports at the time that Charles was a cold, absentee father, this photograph and many others like it, evidence a close, easy relationship.

Photograph by Tim Graham

ETONIAN: Above, in September 1995, Wills, age thirteen, entered Eton College, the elite, 570-year-old boarding school across the River Thames from Windsor Castle. On Sundays after chapel, the prince routinely walked across the bridge and up to the castle to have tea with his grandmother, Queen Elizabeth. The school uniform of black tailcoat, vest, white tie and pinstriped trousers is not just for formal occasions. William and his fellow Etonians also wore "Eton dress" to class.

Photograph by Tim Graham

KILTIE PLEASURE: Right, the Windsor men view Balmoral's Falls of Muick. This 49,000-acre Scottish estate owned by the queen has been a Windsor summer retreat since Queen Victoria and Prince Albert purchased it in 1852. But in 1997, the princes' summer holiday would be cut short. Two weeks after this photograph was taken while the boys were still enjoying Balmoral, their mother, Princess Diana, would perish in a Paris auto accident.

Photograph by Tim Graham

THE PEOPLE'S PRINCES: Above, five days after Princess Diana's death, Charles, William, and Harry flew from Scotland to London. They drove straight to Kensington Palace, where hundreds of thousands of mourners had left massive drifts of flowers, cellophane, and scrawled messages of condolence against the ornate palace gates. In their grief the young princes mustered the poise to gracefully acknowledge the mourners. **Left**, the next day, **l–r**, Prince Philip; Prince William; Diana's brother, Charles; Prince Harry and Prince Charles walked shoulder to shoulder behind Diana's casket during the procession from St. James Palace to Westminster Abbey. "I'm not going to march in any bloody parade," protested a grief-stricken Prince William. His seventy-six-year-old grandfather Prince Philip stepped in: "If I walk," he asked, "will you walk with me?" Wills agreed. An estimated one million pilgrims gathered to say goodbye to Diana; more than two billion watched on television.

Photographs by Tim Graham (left) and Ken Goff (above)

FINAL JOURNEY: Above, following the funeral service at Westminster Abbey, Princess Diana begins the journey to her final resting place, a small wooded island in the center of an ornamental lake at Althorp, the ancestral Spencer home in Lincolnshire. Atop the coffin, draped with the Royal Standard of the United Kingdom, are white tulips and lilies—as well as a small bouquet of cream roses encircled by pink roses accompanied by Prince Harry's handwritten card that says simply "Mummy."

Photograph by Jayne Fincher

POP STAR: Right, William and Harry returned to their respective schools, Eton and Ludgrove, four days after their mother's burial. William, a natural leader, was elected to the school's elite Eton Society of Prefects, also known as "Pop"—an honor at a school that has educated nineteen British prime ministers.

WILLSMANIA: In March 1998, Prince Charles took the boys on a ski holiday to British Columbia on Canada's west coast. While the skiing at Whistler, **left**, was fine, the teenage prince got his first taste of "Willsmania" at a handful of public appearances in nearby Vancouver. Harry kidded his older brother about his newly acquired teen-idol status, but Wills was genuinely disconcerted by the hordes of screaming girls, **above**, and vowed never to go on "walkabout"—a royal meet-and-greet with the public—again. It was a vow he would not be allowed to keep.

Photographs by Tim Graham (left) and Carlo Allegri (above)

A-LEVELS: Above, in June, 2000, during his last month at Eton, Wills prepares for his final exams and A-levels—academically rigorous tests required for university entrance. By virtue of his lineage, Wills could likely attend any university he chose. But as his cousin and fellow Etonian Nicky Knatchbull explained at the time, "He wants to earn it. He doesn't want to have everything handed to him when other people have to work for it. He has too much pride for that."

Photograph by Ken Goff

ROYAL HEARTTHROB: Right, by his sixteenth year, Wills had shot up to over six feet tall. He had become his statuesque mother's strikingly handsome son, with the same fair coloring, dewy complexion, and shy, out-from-under gaze. This photo was snapped during a public appearance after Christmas Day services at Sandringham Church, Norfolk, in 1998.

Photograph by Tim Graham

NEW MILLENNIUM: To celebrate William's eighteenth birthday on June 21, 2000, the Crown Dependency of Jersey issued this set of commemorative stamps depicting the prince's passion for polo and skiing, Caernarfon Castle in Wales, and the new millennium—marked by a fireworks display.

Photograph by Ken Goff

GAP YEAR: Facing page, the future king spent part of his "gap year" between Eton and university in remote coastal Chile, far from his polo-playing, night-clubbing pals. The trip was organized through an adventure travel and good-works charity. Alongside fellow volunteers and a number of at-risk youth, the strapping young prince spent ten weeks with minimal creature comforts, rising early in the morning to chop wood, scour toilets, and paint houses in the tiny coastal village of Tortel. The post he lugs, **top right**, will be lashed onto an elevated walkway; his hammering, **bottom right**, will yield a rubbish bin. William reveled in his off-the-beaten-track freedom and frankly expressed his fear that this Chilean adventure would be as close as his royal life would ever get to normal.

Photographs by Toby Melville

BACK IN THE SADDLE: Home from his gap-year travels abroad, Prince William resumed his hereditary pastimes, including summer polo at Cirencester, near Highgrove, his father's Gloucestershire estate.

Photograph by Tim Graham

QUEEN MUM AT 101: Right, the formidable Windsor men—William, Harry, and Charles—pay tribute to their more formidable "Gran Gran," the queen mother, on the occasion of her 101st birthday in August 2001. The much beloved Elizabeth would pass away seven months later—at the time the longest-lived and perhaps best-loved royal in modern history.

Photograph by Sion Touhig

ST. ANDREWS: His mother's family was all Oxford, and his dad and Uncle Edward attended Cambridge, so which would it be for Wills? As it turned out, neither. The queen, whose own mother was a Scottish thistle through and through, liked the idea of a Scottish university to shore up the royal franchise north of the border. So she was delighted when William became the first heir apparent to matriculate at the University of St. Andrews, Scotland's oldest college (founded in 1413). William was delighted too. He wanted to study art history and St. Andrews had a top-flight program; he would spend his college year far removed from the public glare of Oxbridge, and the beloved Windsor family estate, Balmoral, was only two hours away. Once word of William's matriculation was announced, applications to St. Andrews spiked—particularly from young women. **Left**, a photo op of father and son arriving on campus. **Above**, Wills at a September 21, 2001, press conference in Edinburgh two days before he registered at St. Andrews.

Photograph by Toby Melville (above)

ENTER KATE

The Rise of a Modern Princess

Many young girls dream of growing up and marrying the Prince of Wales. Miss Catherine Elizabeth Middleton of Bucklebury, Berkshire, claims she wasn't one of them. In November 2010, when ITN interviewer Tom Bradby quizzed her, post-engagement announcement, about the too-good-to-be-true reports that she once kept a poster of bonny Prince William tacked to her bedroom wall, the newly affianced Kate replied with her usual charm: "He wishes. No, I had the Levis guy on my wall, not a picture of William. Sorry." But countless British girls, Canadian girls, Australian girls, and even some American girls *did* keep pictures of handsome Prince William in their rooms. And there is little in Kate's family background to suggest that she, amongst all the girls in the world, would marry the heartthrob heir to the British throne.

The last time a future king married a commoner was a mere three-and-a-half centuries ago—in 1660, when Anne Hyde, daughter of a prominent court politician, married the future King James II. A few caveats here: First of all, Anne was pregnant at the time; second, no one expected James to ever become king, and third, Ann died before she became queen—though she did give birth to two future British monarchs. Much later, in 1937, Edward VIII married American commoner Wallis Simpson, but he abdicated the throne to do it.

The point is, this sort of thing doesn't happen very often. Royalty marries royalty, or at least, other aristocrats. And in a society still constrained by class distinctions, the presumptive Queen Catherine's family is solidly middle class. Middle class with money—but in Britain, money doesn't make an aristocrat.

WINNING SMILE: Kate Middleton, Prince William's future bride, in Dublin, Ireland, April 2007.
Photograph by Aidan Crawley

Kate's parents, Michael and Carole Middleton, met in the mid-1970s when they both worked for British Airways at London's Heathrow Airport. (He checked aircraft before departure; she was a flight attendant.) Michael, the Leeds-born son of an airline pilot, was soon promoted to flight dispatcher, and when Michael and Carole married, they bought a modest home near Reading, forty miles west of London. The Middletons had three children: Kate in 1982, Pippa a year later, and James in 1987. From May 1984 until September 1987, the Middletons lived in Amman, Jordan, where Kate attended nursery school and learned rudimentary Arabic. When they returned to the UK, Michael and Carole founded a family business — a small mail-order party supply company called Party Pieces. When they shrewdly adapted their enterprise to the Internet, Party Pieces succeeded beyond expectation.

In 1995, Michael and Carole were able to purchase an attractive five-bedroom brick home on an acre of land in the Berkshire village of Bucklebury. And when Catherine — she was Catherine then — and her siblings reached middle school age, the Middletons were sufficiently well heeled to send them to tony £15,000-per-year Marlborough College — alma mater of film star James Mason, the traitor Anthony Blunt, a raft of British politicians, and the occasional royal. There, Catherine flourished. She was captain of the field hockey team, a star tennis player and high jumper, an excellent student, and an all-around popular girl. A former classmate recalls her as "level-headed and down-to-earth, an absolutely phenomenal girl — really popular, talented, creative and sporty." A former teacher adds, "She was universally liked and to top it all she was a joy to teach. Quite sickening, really."

When Catherine left Marlborough as Kate, she did what Prince William did — took a gap year before starting her art history studies at the University of St. Andrews. William roughed it in rural Chile. Coincidentally, Kate volunteered in Chile, too, but she also sailed off the Isle of Wight and enjoyed several months in Florence soaking up the masterpieces of the Italian Renaissance. When she arrived at St. Andrews in September 2001, Kate was assigned to the female section of St. Salvator's Hall, nicknamed "Sally's." Prince William found rooms in the male quarters and would soon notice the athletic (like him), outdoorsy (like him), art history major (like him, at the time) whom the boys crowned "the prettiest girl in Sally's."

THE MIDDLETONS OF BUCKLEBURY: Kate Middleton's parents, Michael and Carole, met when both worked for British Airways at London's Heathrow Airport. When their mail-order party supply business, Party Pieces, went online, the Middletons hit the jackpot. **Top**, Oak Acre, the Middletons' comfortable five-bedroom home near Bucklebury, Berkshire, photographed in 2004. **Bottom**, the Middletons in 2010.

FAMILY ALBUM: As a youngster, Catherine Middleton was cheerful and determined. In photographs from the Middleton family album, we see Catherine, **above**, at age three-and-a-half, rock climbing in England's Lake District; **facing page**, **top**, probably at age four, visiting classical ruins with sister, Pippa, sometime during the two-and-a-half years their father worked in Amman, Jordan: and, **facing page**, **bottom**, when she was five years old, in 1987.

PLAYING TO WIN: Before she attended posh Marlborough College, Catherine Middleton went to St. Andrew's Preparatory School, four miles from her home. As her yearbook photos attest, she soon blossomed into a star athlete proficient at tennis, hockey, swimming, rounders (a forerunner of baseball), and netball (a derivation of basketball). She also played Eliza Doolittle in the St. Andrew's production of *My Fair Lady*, learned ballet and tap, and was a skilled singer and flautist. **Above**, the future princess was St. Andrew's highest scorer in rounders. **Left**, Catherine in her class photo, circa 1995.

ANOTHER VICTORY: Young Catherine celebrates a field hockey conquest at St. Andrew's. The athletic Middleton would continue to excel at field hockey and develop into a star cross-country runner when she left St. Andrew's to attend elite Marlborough College.

AUSPICIOUS MOMENT: Near the end of his freshman year at the University of St. Andrews, Prince William attended the school's annual student-run charity fashion show. Wills paid £200 for his front-row seat, and Kate sizzled on the catwalk in a series of revealing outfits. Said one fellow student, "We were all wowed. Here was this reserved girl we knew up on stage looking like a smoldering temptress." Wills took note. Soon after, when he and his old Eton chum Fergus Boyd scouted off-campus lodgings for their sophomore year, they invited Kate (who had a boyfriend at the time) to join them.

PASSING OF THE MATRIARCH: Left, two days into their 2002 ski holiday in Klosters, Switzerland, Prince Charles and his sons received the news that Elizabeth, the queen mother (William and Harry's great-grandmother, Charles's grandmother and the mother of Queen Elizabeth), had passed away at the age of 101. Devastated by the news, they rushed home. **Above**, Prince Charles, Prince William, and Prince Philip follow the coffin of the Queen Mum, as she was affectionately called, in procession from St James's Palace to Westminster Hall for the lying in state.

Photographs by Julian Herbert (left) and Tim Graham (above)

COUNTRY KIDS: Following pages, long before it was fashionable, Prince Charles threw his royal weight behind sustainable organic farming and animal husbandry. Once mocked for admitting that he talked to his vegetables, Charles became a leading figure in the international "slow food" movement, which he practices on 15 acres at Highgrove and 1,100 acres at Duchy Home Farm in Gloucestershire. Wills, who shares his father's passion, holds an organically raised lamb at Highgrove. Kate strikes a pose at the annual Game Fair held at Blenheim Palace in Oxfordshire.

Photographs by Tim Graham (following pages, left) and Stephen Lock (following pages, right)

*I just want to go to
university and have
fun. I want to be an
ordinary student.*

—PRINCE WILLIAM

MAKING A GO OF IT: During his first year at St. Andrews, Wills became disaffected both with the university and with his chosen course of study, art history. He wanted to drop out, but as with everything he did, the prince had to consider the public-relations consequences. If he left St. Andrews after a year, the venerable university would have been wounded by the perceived royal insult, and at least for a while, the prince would be branded a quitter. Prince Charles weighed in, urging his son to stick it out. William's friend, Kate Middleton, was likewise unhappy. They consoled each other, resolving to make a go of it. Kate also helped with William's decision to shift his major from art history to geography.

Photograph by Tim Graham

MEMBER OF THE CLAN: Kate had already attended the Prince of Wales's fifty-sixth birthday party at Highgrove—a favorable sign—when Charles invited her to join him and his boys on their annual spring ski trip to Klosters, Switzerland, in March, 2005. The trip was Charles's last hurrah as a bachelor before marrying Camilla Parker Bowles the following month. The Prince of Wales also invited Harry's girlfriend, Chelsy Davy, who preferred to stay in South Africa instead. The Alpine weather cooperated, and Kate and Wills were relaxed and openly affectionate. In a few months, their relatively private university days would be over. **Facing page**, Kate outside the lodge. **Left**, Wills posing for the paparazzi. **Above**, Kate, a natural athlete and experienced skier, shows her form.

Photographs by Tim Graham (facing page and left)

TWO WEDDINGS: Above, the wedding of longtime Windsor family friend Hugh Van Cutsem to Rose Astor in June 2005 was the first high-profile social affair that Wills and Kate attended simultaneously—though they were careful not to be photographed together. **Left**, an officially released wedding portrait of the Prince of Wales and his new bride, Camilla, Duchess of Cornwall, with their families in Windsor Castle's White Drawing Room after their wedding ceremony on April 9, 2005. **L–r**, standing, are Prince Harry, Prince William, the groom, the bride, and Tom and Laura Parker Bowles, Camilla's children from her first marriage. **L–r**, seated, are the groom's parents, the Duke of Edinburgh and HM Queen Elizabeth II and the bride's father Major Bruce Shand. "We are both very happy for our father and Camilla, and we wish them all the luck in the future," said Wills and Harry in a prepared statement. "We love her to bits," Harry told a reporter more informally.

Photograph by Hugo Burnand (left)

GRADUATION: The University of St. Andrews had never seen anything quite like its 594th graduation exercises on June 23, 2005, when degrees were awarded to both Prince William, second in line to the British throne, and his girlfriend Kate Middleton. Despite feeling under the weather, Queen Elizabeth attended her first family graduation, where she also had the opportunity to meet Kate's parents for the first time.

MILITARY MANEUVERS: Prince Harry skipped university altogether and went directly to the Royal Military Academy at Sandhurst. So when William also decided to tackle Sandhurst's rigorous forty-four-week officer training program, he found himself following in his younger brother's footsteps. During the gap months between his university graduation and the start of his military training, William traveled to New Zealand as the queen's representative, to Kenya on safari with Kate and friends, and to Klosters for his third annual ski trip with Kate. He also spent two weeks learning about estate management at Chatsworth, the 35,000-acre seat of the Duke of Devonshire, and three weeks in London getting "work experience" with HSBC, an international bank. But William's career interest was definitely bending toward the military. On January 8, 2006, at age 23, Officer Cadet Wales entered Sandhurst for his eleven-month officer-training course. **Left**, prepping for Sandhurst, the prince visits the army's Regular Commissions Board in Wiltshire for a series of interviews and physical tests to assess his personality and leadership skills. **Above**, Wills trains with the RAF Valley Mountain Rescue Team on the Welsh island of Anglesey in December 2005. William would return to Anglesey to live with Kate after their wedding.

Photograph by Tim Graham (above)

BETWIXT AND BETWEEN: By 2005 Prince William's career path was largely laid out for him; Kate's was less clear. After graduating from St. Andrews, she moved into her parents' one-bedroom pied-à-terre in London's Chelsea district. As the prince's girlfriend, she lived a double life, hovering, as one biographer put it, "half in and half out of the royal family." When she was with William, Kate was safeguarded by the Royalty Protection Branch and treated, more or less, like a princess. The rest of the time she was on her own, riding public buses and looking for an art gallery job. **Left**, Kate's sensational style was on display during the horse trials at the Festival of British Eventing held at Gatcombe Park, Princess Anne's estate in Gloucestershire, August 6, 2005. **Above**, Kate and her mother, Carole Middleton, shop at the Spirit of Christmas Fair at London's Olympia hall in November of the same year.

YES OR NO: Following pages, in the hothouse atmosphere of a family wedding—William's stepsister, Laura Parker Bowles, to Harry Lopes in May 2006—everyone wondered if the two freshly tanned, just-back-from-Mustique superstars in their midst would soon make a big announcement.

PART OF THE FAMILY: Above left, after Kate's impromptu and unaccompanied appearance in the royal box for the 2006 Cheltenham races, London bookies lowered the odds against a royal marriage. The spectacle of Kate casually dropping in on Prince Charles and Camilla at one of the Duchess of Cornwall's highest-profile events was unusual. But when Camilla warmly welcomed her, it sealed the impression that Kate was now an accepted member of a new, more relaxed, royal family: "Here was a rag-tag group," wrote royal watcher Robert Jobson (who introduces this book), "each member with a tale to tell: some of marital strife and infidelity, some of young love, some of privilege squandered but recovered." **Above right**, the day after the Cheltenham races, William and Kate reunite at Eton's Old Boys Field Game with a rare public display of affection.

Photograph by Tim Graham (above, left)

WAR GAMES: Facing page, Officer Cadet Wales takes part in the "Winter Victory" field exercises at Paramali village, Cyprus, on November 20, 2006. This would be his last test before he was commissioned as a British officer.

Photograph by Corporal Ian Houlding

A MAN IN UNIFORM: On December 15, 2006, Kate Middleton and Her Majesty the Queen traveled, separately, to Berkshire to watch Cadet Wales "pass out" (graduate) from the Royal Military Academy Sandhurst. Like brother Harry, who preceded him by a few months, William was commissioned into the Household Cavalry's Blues and Royals regiment. "I love the uniform!" Kate, **left**, reportedly whispered to her mother as the prince marched by with a rifle on his shoulder and a crimson sash across his black wool uniform, "It's so, so sexy." **Above**, as titular head of the armed forces, the queen inspects her grandson's raiment with a more critical eye—apparently to his amusement.

Photographs by Tim Graham (left) and Adrian Dennis (above)

LIFE IN THE FISHBOWL: During their university days, the press agreed to leave the prince and his girlfriend alone. But upon their graduation, the deal was off. These photographs were taken in a matter of minutes as Kate Middleton left her Chelsea flat to work at her new job as an accessories buyer for retail fashion chain Jigsaw. It was the morning of her twenty-fifth birthday, January 9, 2007, but it wasn't just her birthday. The weekly *Spectator* had just published "The Next People's Princess," wherein Patrick Jephson, Princess Diana's former private secretary, suggested that a royal engagement was imminent. Worldwide pressure for photos was on. In response, Prince William issued an unusual official statement saying he wanted "more than anything" for Kate to be left alone.

PUBLIC AFFAIR: After years of taking great pains not to be photographed together in public, William and Kate seemed to let their guard down a bit in early 2007. **Left**, the prince and his girlfriend cheer on the English rugby team against Italy during the Six Nations Championship at Twickenham Stadium, aka "Twickers," on February 10, 2007. **Above**, the couple finds time for a Zermatt ski trip during William's ten-month tank-command training in Dorset. But as the couple was photographed together more often, they were actually spending more time apart.

Photograph by Richard Heathcote (left)

A DAY AT THE RACES: By the time the Cheltenham races rolled around again in March 2007, royal watchers had their microscopes out, looking for hairline fractures on the smooth façade of William and Kate's romance. The tabloids had recently printed pictures of the 24-year-old prince out clubbing with several pretty girls, and Kate's patience was tried. **Above**, Prince William and Kate attended the first day of the Cheltenham Festival in Gloucestershire together, but, **right**, Kate returns with other friends three days later.

Photograph by Eddie Keogh (right)

THE SPLIT: On April 14, 2007, the *Sun* broke the news that Prince William and Kate Middleton had called it quits. The BBC confirmed the story later that day. Noting the previously widespread speculation about an impending engagement, the BBC's royal correspondent, Nicholas Witchell, commented that the breakup was "a surprise, because [the relationship] had seemed very stable and very steady." The *Daily Mail* was less circumspect, branding the prince as "selfish, self-centred, and careless of history.... In Kate Middleton, the most grounded woman to set foot in a Royal court in several generations, the nation has lost a future Queen who would have brought lustre and stability to the Royal Family." Clarence House, the prince's official residence and public relations office, offered its usual terse statement: "We don't comment on Prince William's private life."

KEEPING HER COOL: William and Kate had separated briefly during their university days, but now the stakes were higher, with their romance... and breakup... played out on Britain's front pages. **Top,** Kate, pictured three days before the bombshell hit, deftly said nothing at all, and continued to work at the fashion chain Jigsaw's head office. **Bottom,** the chain's King's Road location in London.

ALEXIA GOETHE GALLER
7 DOVER STREET LONDON W1S
WWW.ALEXIAGOETHEGALLERY
INFO@GOETHEGALLERY.COM | 00 44 (0) 207-6

DAY TO FRIDAY   10AM
DAY   11AM

THE SINGLETON: If Kate Middleton was devastated by the royal breakup, she never showed it. In the weeks following the announcement, she was a fixture at London's hottest nightspots—Mahiki, Kitts Club, Raffles, and Boujis—always looking toned and ravishing. She attended book launches and horse trials, and traveled to the playground island of Ibiza. "It has become a much remarked oddity of Kate and Prince William's break-up," noted the *Daily Mail*, "that, in the weeks since her apparent heartbreak, she has never looked better…or happier."

THE SIZZLE SISTERS: For company, Kate often enlisted her younger sister, Pippa, **above right**, who had just ended a two-year relationship with banking heir JJ Jardine Paterson. Variously dubbed the "Wisteria Sisters" ("decorative, fragrant, with great ability to climb") or the less-snarky "Sizzle Sisters" (by *Tatler* magazine), the Middleton girls became must-have guests in young London's social circles. As the *Daily Mail* put it, "If Kate Middleton's aim is to take revenge on her former boyfriend for dumping her, things could hardly be going more according to plan."

REMEMBERING MOM: The Concert for Diana at Wembley Stadium, planned and hosted by William and Harry, featured an impressive lineup of star performers, including Elton John, Fergie, and Kanye West. The charity event held on July 1, 2007, celebrated what would have been Diana's forty-sixth birthday. "We wanted to have this big concert full of energy," Prince William said, "full of the sort of fun and happiness which I know she would have wanted. And on her birthday as well, it's got to be the best birthday present she ever had."

The sold-out, six-hour concert was broadcast to 140 countries and watched by millions. **Above**, at a rehearsal, the prince shows singer Joss Stone where he'll be sitting. **Left**, Harry and William, their friends and cousins, do what Brits call a Mexican wave. Kate Middleton sits a row back and to the right of Prince William. Prince Harry's girlfriend, Chelsy Davy, is far left. Since shortly after their breakup, more than two months earlier, the ostensibly separated Will and Kate spoke regularly by phone, and at this point they were secretly dating again.

Photograph by Tim Graham (above)

THE SISTERHOOD: Looking for a fun way to keep fit, Kate joined the Sisterhood, a group of twenty-one women training to row a dragon boat across the English Channel in a one-off challenge race against the Brotherhood, a rival men's team. The Sisterhood billed itself, tongue-in-cheek, as "an elite group of female athletes, talented in many ways, toned to perfection, with killer looks, on a mission to keep boldly going where no girl has gone before." But with Kate's romance reheating, the Sisterhood's practice sessions on the River Thames became a paparazzi magnet. Kate withdrew from the Sisterhood in August 2007 and returned to the confines of royal life—this time for good.

enge.com

THE PRODUCER: By the end of 2007, William and Kate were firmly back in the couple groove. Kate left her job with Jigsaw to devote time to her new passion, photography. She traveled to New York to meet Mario Testino, the well-known celebrity portraitist who shot Princess Diana for the covers of *Vogue* and *Vanity Fair*. (Four years later, he would take the couple's official engagement snaps. See pages 148 and 157.) In November, Kate produced a charity show of celebrity shots by British photographer Alistair Morrison, with proceeds going to UNICEF.

SNOWBIRDS: Like swallows to Capistrano, every March the Windsors fly to the ski resort at Klosters, Switzerland, where one cable car has been officially dubbed "Prince of Wales." Here, William and Kate share a T-bar on March 19, 2008.

FLYBOY: After a four-month course with the Royal Air Force, Prince William joined previous generations of Windsor men as flyers. **Left**, decked out in the gold braid and medals of Air Chief Marshal, Prince Charles congratulates his son after presenting him with his wings during graduation ceremonies at RAF Cranwell on April 11, 2008. Fortunately for the twenty-five-year-old prince, his personal use of $16 million Chinook helicopters—including a landing in the Middleton backyard and a jaunt to the Isle of Wight for a stag weekend—wasn't revealed in the press until a few days later. **Above**, Kate and William after the ceremony.

FIGHT FANS: After training with the British army and the Royal Air Force, the future king attended the Brittania Royal Naval College in Dartmouth during June and July 2008. The "sub-lieutenant" spent his first weekend off with Kate, Prince Harry, Chelsy Davy, and other old friends at the Boodles Boxing Ball at London's Royal Lancaster Hotel. After the standard champagne reception, dinner, and auction, the black-tie charity event featured a series of pugilistic matches between well-heeled Etonians, in the blue corner, and Cambridge graduates in the red. Kate winced as the couple's old friend James Meade took a beating at the hands of Al Poulain, a former equerry to Prince Charles. **Above,** Kate, wore a gown by one of her favorite designers, Brazilian-born Daniella Issa Helayel. **Right**, William and Kate between rounds.

Photographs by Davidson/O'Neill

ORDER OF THE GARTER: The weekend after the Boodles Boxing Ball came another, even grander affair: Garter Day, the 660th Anniversary Service, at St. George's Chapel, Windsor Castle. At this event, Prince William became the one thousandth Knight of the Garter, a member of Britain's oldest chivalric order, founded in 1348 by Edward III. According to the order's medieval rules, there can be no more than twenty-six Knights and Ladies of the Garter at any given time. The second-highest honor in the land (after a peerage), it is considered one of the monarch's few remaining, truly personal, executive prerogatives. **Left**, William in full regalia. Reportedly neither Prince Harry nor Kate, **above**, with the Duchess of Cornwall, could maintain composure when William paraded by in his ostrich-plumed Tudor bonnet.

Photographs by Chris Jackson (left) and Tim Graham (above)

GOOD FUN FOR GOOD CAUSES: Left, Kate creates a stir as she arrives at the Day-Glo Midnight Roller Disco fundraiser in Vauxhall, London. Sensitive to charges that she was a princess-in-waiting with nothing to do, Kate worked in her family's business and used her star power to support charitable fundraisers during this period. The 1980s-themed roller-disco event raised money for the Children's Hospital in Oxford and the Place2Be youth counseling organization.

In the same vein, Princes William and Harry flew south to join the thousand-mile 2008 Enduro Africa Challenge rally that raised $400,000 for the Nelson Mandela Children's Fund, UNICEF, and Sentebale, a charity founded by Prince Harry in memory of his mother. The motocross event took eight days, navigating mostly dirt tracks along the wild, spectacular coast of South Africa's Eastern Cape. **Facing page**, the future king prepares for the start of the rally in Port Edward, KwaZulu-Natal. "It's a mixture of adventure and charity," William told the BBC.

Photographs by Michelly Rall (facing page) and Danny Martindale (left)

REMEMBERING THE FALLEN: On an official visit to the National Memorial Arboretum in Staffordshire, Prince William recognized two names inscribed in stone: Major Alexis Roberts, of the First Battalion, Royal Ghurka Rifles, his former platoon commander at Sandhurst, who was killed in Afghanistan; and Intelligence Officer Joanna Dyer who trained with the prince and was killed near Basra in Iraq.

Photograph by Christopher Furlong

POLO SEASON: **Above**, the prince and Kate appear together publicly for the first time in five months at a charity polo event at Coworth Park Polo Club in Berkshire, May 2009. The prince had been in North Shropshire completing his RAF rescue helicopter course. He managed to slip away most weekends, but the couple's time together was still limited. **Right**, a few weeks later, William plays in the Dorchester Trophy match during a downpour at Cirencester—on the very field where his polo-loving father broke his arm in a 1990 fall. The Prince of Wales retired from the game in 2005, at age fifty-seven, leaving the field to his two talented sons.

CHOPPER PILOT: In September 2008, Clarence House made the surprise announcement that Prince William, fresh from a summer with the Royal Navy, would join the RAF as a search and rescue pilot. In practice, this meant he could postpone his official duties as Prince of the Realm for at least five years. He would continue his charity work, but his primary job was now military: "Joining search and rescue," he said, "is a perfect opportunity for me to serve in the forces operationally." The prince returned to RAF Shawbury for additional training, then transferred to RAF Valley on the isle of Anglesey, Wales, to complete his nineteen-month course. Upon graduation, he accepted a full-time, three-year posting at the same base with the RAF Search and Rescue Force as co-pilot in a four-man rescue helicopter flying missions all across the United Kingdom. His unit, "C" Flight of 22 Squadron, logged 322 rescues in 2009. **Right**, Flight lieutenant Wales at the helm of a Griffin helicopter in June 2009.

WEDDING BELLS: Following pages, Prince William and Kate Middleton attend the wedding of old family friend Nicholas van Cutsem to Alice Hadden-Paton, at The Guards Chapel, Wellington Barracks, London, August 14, 2009.

DOWN UNDER: Representing his grandmother the queen, William made his first state visit abroad to New Zealand to dedicate that country's new, $80 million Supreme Court building in Wellington on January 18, 2010. The queen and Prince Philip, both well past eighty, had decided to cut back their foreign travel. So young Prince William, left to his own devices, had to carefully calibrate his visit to a proud, modern country divided on the question of monarchical versus republican government. The prince decided that, more than anything, he should avoid pomp. Instead, he enjoyed no less than four barbecues. **Above**, William greets Sir Paul Reeves, the country's first Maori governor-general, with a traditional Polynesian hongi, wherein the "ha," or breath of life, is shared. **Right**, William's antipodean trip included a quick, unofficial two-day visit to Australia. Here, he arrives at Government House in Melbourne where "Willsmania" was still in evidence. All in all, the trip was a smashing success. The morning William left for Hong Kong, Melbourne's *Herald Sun* stacked its racks with a special souvenir edition of the prince's visit. The cover headline: "Mum Would Be Proud."

Photographs by Brendon O'Hagan (above) and Scott Barbour (right)

GOOD COMPANY: On the 350th anniversary of the Royal Society, Prince William was inducted as an Honorary Fellow in the presence of his grandparents, the queen and Prince Philip. The oldest scientific organization in Great Britain, the Society is "a fellowship of the world's most eminent scientists… that aim[s] to expand the frontiers of knowledge by championing the development and use of science, mathematics, engineering and medicine for the benefit of humanity and the good of the planet." The prince's remarks were appropriately modest. "I have to say that if I look at the names of some of the Society's great Fellows—Boyle, Newton, Banks, Darwin and our current president, Lord Rees—butterflies do flutter in my stomach a little."

Photograph by Akira Suemori

WE'VE GOT A SECRET: Three weeks before they publicly announced their engagement, William and Kate attended the wedding of William's childhood pal Harry Meade to primary school teacher Rosie Bradford, in Gloucestershire. Wills and Kate surprised the gossip press when they arrived at the church together, but the public was as yet unaware that they were secretly engaged. **Above**, bride Rosie Bradford arrives at the Gloucestershire church in a vintage Rolls Royce. **Right**, just back from a Kenyan safari, Prince William brings his clandestine fiancée, Kate Middleton, to see his old partner-in-crime get hitched.

Photograph by Tim Rooke (right)

THE ENGAGEMENT

After eight years, her patience is rewarded

At last. That was the sentiment expressed by the prospective groom's grandmother, the queen of England. More precisely, Her Majesty said, "It has taken them a very long time." That view was echoed by William's father, Prince Charles, who quipped to a BBC reporter, "They've been practicing long enough." Perhaps not surprisingly, the prospective bride's father, Michael Middleton, put a shinier gloss on his daughter's protracted romance. In his prepared statement to the reporters clustered outside his Berkshire home, he said, "As you know, Catherine and Prince William have been going out together for quite a number of years, which is great for us, because we have gotten to know William very well." As for Kate's mum, well, she let her husband do the talking, but the expression on her face — described by Britain's *Daily Mail* as a "perma-smile"— said it all.

After eight years, at least two breakups, several false engagement alarms, and perhaps millions of speculative words in the media, most of Britain and a fair portion of the world breathed a collective sigh of relief when, on November 16, 2010, Prince Charles's office issued a proclamation stating simply: "The Prince of Wales is delighted to announce the engagement of Prince William to Miss Catherine Middleton." The typically terse Clarence House statement, released simultaneously on Facebook and Twitter, further reported that the wedding would take place in London during "the Spring or Summer of 2011," that Prince William and Miss Middleton had become engaged a month earlier in Kenya, and quaintly, that Prince William, "had sought the permission of Miss Middleton's father."

OFFICIAL ENGAGEMENT PORTRAIT: Facing page, one of two official portraits of the newly-engaged Prince William and Kate Middleton taken on November 25, 2010, by celebrity photographer Mario Testino and released by Clarence House, December 12, 2010.

It stands to reason that after an eight-year courtship, Mr. Middleton might grant his permission quickly and with great enthusiasm, but apparently Prince William was not fully confident of the result. "I was torn between asking Kate's dad first," said the prince during an ITV interview shortly after the engagement was announced, "and then the realization that he might actually say no dawned upon me. So I thought if I ask Kate first, then he can't really say no. So I did it that way round."

When, hours after the announcement the newly affianced couple entered the State Apartments of St. James's Palace to meet the press (see photos on pages 152–155), Prince William was decked out in a bespoke blue suit by Gieves & Hawkes of Savile Row, royal tailors for two centuries, and Kate was resplendent in a — let's call it royal blue — Issa dress. Thousands of flash bursts illuminated the moment.

Within hours, Kate's £399 ($650) silk jersey dress sold out of every shop in London, but the real star of the event was lodged on the fourth finger of the prospective bride's left hand. Kate's eighteen-carat oval blue sapphire and diamond dazzler (see a close-up on page 155) was immediately recognizable as the ring that William's mother, Lady Diana, selected for her own engagement three decades earlier. In 1981, the ring was available from a catalog — albeit a very pricey Garrard of Mayfair catalog — for around $65,000, but in 2010 its royal provenance had boosted the ring's value to nearly $500,000.

And what a provenance it has: Princess Diana continued to wear the ring during her separation and even after her divorce. It appears in countless photos. When she died suddenly and tragically in 1997, William and Harry were each allowed to select a few mementos from the late princess's possessions. William, age fifteen, chose Diana's gold Cartier tank watch and Harry, age twelve, selected his mother's famous ring.

At some point, Harry apparently agreed that the ring should grace the hand of the future queen of England, so he passed title to William. Prior to his October trip to Kenya with Kate, William removed the ring from a royal safe in the Queen's living quarters at Buckingham Palace, and then carefully conveyed it around Africa in his knapsack for three weeks before offering it to his girlfriend. Whether the future king did so on bended knee is a matter for speculation. At the photo call, William parried the question, and Kate would only add demurely that the moment was "very romantic."

Some royal observers have questioned William's decision to repurpose his mother's ring. For some, it's hard to forget that the last time this particular piece of jewelry was employed for the same purpose, the marriage ended rather badly. But William has no such qualms. "Obviously [my mother] is not going to be around to share any of the fun and excitement," said the prince during his post-engagement interview. "This was my way of keeping her close to it all."

The prince's optimism, what Samuel Johnson long ago termed "the triumph of hope over experience," was echoed in the marketplace. Minutes after the ring was revealed to reporters and photographers, jewelry stores around the world were besieged with frantic calls for less expensive knockoffs. Michael Arnstein, the CEO of New York's Natural Sapphire Co., told the *Today Show*, "We're in a frenzy. This is changing our business overnight." Arnstein then remembered that the same phenomenon occurred when the ring was initially unveiled in 1981. Which all goes to show that Diana, "the people's princess," was anointed a style icon for a reason, and that in this regard, whether she likes it or not, Kate Middleton, the first commoner to marry a future king in more than three-and-a-half centuries, may be her heir.

PHOTO OP: Following pages, Prince William and Kate Middleton at the official photo call following the public announcement of their engagement in the State Apartments of St. James's Palace, November 16, 2010. In an interview with ITV News later that day, the interviewer remarked that the couple seemed "incredibly happy and relaxed."

"We are," the prince replied. "We're sort of like ducks, very calm on the surface, with our little feet going under the water." The couple's plans called for the most elaborate royal wedding since William's parents married in 1981.

Photograph by Ben Stansall

WILLIAM'S WIT: "I'm extremely funny and she loves that, so it's been good," observed Prince William about his durable eight-year affair with Kate. **Above**, Kate appreciates one of William's quips at the St. James's photo call on November 16, 2010.

Photograph by Ben Stansall

KATE'S ROCK: Kate shows off the famous sapphire-and-diamond engagement ring that once belonged to Princess Diana. It went for £28,000 ($65,000) in 1981, but was worth close to half a million dollars in 2010. The prince proposed to Kate, ring in hand, while on holiday in Kenya. "I had been carrying it around with me in my rucksack for about three weeks before that, and I literally would not let it go. Everywhere I went I was keeping hold of it because I knew this thing, if it disappeared, I would be in a lot of trouble."

Photograph by Tim Rooke

MEET THE PRESS: Above, during William and Kate's post-engagement interview, ITV journalist Tom Bradby asked Kate, "Does William ever cook or indeed do anything useful around the house?" William intervened slyly: "Define useful, Tom." Bradby replied: "Let's not go there." Then Kate charmingly suggested that the future king was pretty much a disaster in the kitchen. **Right**, another, less formal, but still official, engagement portrait of Prince William and Kate Middleton.

Photograph by Mario Testino (right)

They make a lovely couple, they're great fun to be with, and we've had a lot of laughs together. We wish them every happiness for the future.

— MICHAEL MIDDLETON TO THE PRESS ON THE DAY
OF HIS DAUGHTER'S ENGAGEMENT ANNOUNCEMENT

JOYFUL PARENTS: Back in Bucklebury, there was un-alloyed delight at the long-awaited engagement news. The bride-to-be's parents, Michael and Carole Middleton, appeared outside their home to make a statement. "We all think he's wonderful," said Mr. Middleton of his prospective son-in-law, "and we're extremely fond of him." Prince Charles, speaking to the BBC, was some-what more wry, quipping, "They've been practicing for long enough."

Photograph by Stefan Rousseau

It means I get a sister, which I have always wanted.

— PRINCE HARRY REACTING TO NEWS OF
HIS BROTHER'S ENGAGEMENT

FRONT-PAGE NEWS: Word of the engagement was splashed across every front page in the kingdom. Reaction came from other quarters, as well: "It is brilliant news," the queen told a guest at a Windsor Castle reception for leaders of British overseas territories. Prime Minister David Cameron reported that when he shared the news with his cabinet, there was a burst of cheers and applause. "It's great to have a bit of unadulterated good news," said the prime minister, who was readying his new austerity program for rollout across the United Kingdom. Of course, not everyone was as optimistic: "If she were my sister, I'd tell her to get a good prenup," sniffed Patrick Jephson, Princess Diana's former private secretary.

Photograph by Ben Stansall

a cape then? Trends that die
G2 Page 14

DAILY Mirror
November 17, 2010
Kate
FREE INSIDE
8-page royal engagement souvenir edit
ROYAL NEWS... ROYAL ENTERTAINMENT 45p

the guardian

Royal wedding in the age of austerity Kate and William to marry

Prince William announced that they had become engaged on holiday in Kenya in October. They will marry next year Photograph: Ben Stansall/AFP

Jonathan Freedland

WITH THIS RING

Inside Kate and William— souvenir edition Plus Tin

THE TIME

Wednesday, November 17 2010 | thetimes.co.uk | No 70107

The new romantic

Something borrowed, something blue: Diana's ring seals royal engage

Valentine Low

FINANCIAL TIMES

Wednesday November 17 2010 | £2.00

Sponsoring equality
Sylvia Hewlett on a woman's path to the top. Comment, Page 15

What happens when a start-up grows up
Judgment call, Page 16

G

Rescue team sets up talks in Dublin

UK considers billions in loans for neighbour
Aid 'not inevitable' says Irish finance minister

By Peter Spiegel and James Chaffin in Brussels and George Parker in London

Royal union Prince William to wed

Shadow banks to face global scrutiny, says Turner

By Patrick Jenkins and Brooke Masters

A seven-year hitch
10 pages of the best news, analysis and pictures
pages 4-15
Leading article, page 2
Alice Thomson, page 30
David Aaronovitch, page 30

Kate Middleton and Prince William at St James's Palace yesterday. He said the ring was his way of making sure that his mother didn't miss out on

Continued on page 4, col 4

Royal engagement **16 pages of souvenir coverage**

The Daily Telegraph

NEWSPAPER OF THE YEAR   Irish Republic €1.20   No 48,354

November 17, 2010

Kate's very special

ce's verdict on his bride-to-be – and that's why she deserved his mother's rir

By Richard Palmer
Royal Correspondent

DELIGHTED Prince William told last night how he proposed to Kate Middleton using Princess Diana's engagement ring.

A token of love in

COIN OF THE REALM: On December 22, 2010, the British Royal Mint issued the first coin ever to commemorate a royal engagement. Although both Prince William and the queen apparently approved the design, the mint's less-than-flattering depiction of the newly-affianced couple on its £5 "Alderney coin" (officially issued by the Channel Island of Alderney) met with nearly universal derision. Nevertheless, the mint issued a limited edition of fifty thousand "brilliant uncirculated" copper-nickel coins in commemorative folders for £9.95, fifteen thousand sterling silver coins for £55.50, and for true enthusiasts, one thousand copies of its solid gold version for a mere £1,550 ($2,529) apiece.

CHINA PLATES: At the Tangshan Hengrui Porcelain Company, 110 miles east of Beijing, a worker inspects commemorative plates to be sold in British souvenir shops. Only days after the announcement, all manner of royal wedding souvenirs, from T-shirts to tea towels to condoms, were offered for sale across Britain and the world. Even the British Monarchy got in on the act, offering "the official Royal Wedding range" of English fine bone china "approved by the couple."

HOME SWEET HOME: Scenes from the Isle of Anglesey, off the coast of northern Wales, where Royal Air Force Flight Lieutenant William Wales and his new wife will be stationed until 2013. **Top**, the entrance to RAF Valley, where Prince William has served as a rescue helicopter pilot since September 2010. **Bottom**, the main shopping street in Holyhead (population 13,000), Anglesey County's largest town.

Photographs by Christopher Furlong

GETTING OFF ON THE RIGHT FOOT: Prince William and future Anglesonian Catherine Middleton, **right**, chose Anglesey for their first official joint appearance. They dedicated a Royal National Lifeboat Institution rescue craft on windblown Trearddur Bay. Kate, in a stylish feather "fascinator" adorned with a badge of the Royal Welsh Fusiliers, delighted the crowd when she sang the Welsh national anthem, "Hen Wlad Fy Nhadau."

Photograph by Dylan Martinez

BACK WHERE IT ALL BEGAN: The affianced couple's second official engagement was a triumphant return to the University of St. Andrews, where they met nearly a decade earlier. William and Catherine helped launch their alma mater's six-hundredth-anniversary celebration, and the university returned the favor, announcing a £70,000 scholarship to celebrate the royal wedding. **Above**, crowds line the streets of St. Andrews awaiting a glimpse of the royal couple. **Facing page**, William and Kate stroll with the Right Honourable Sir Walter Menzies Campbell, university chancellor and member of the British parliament.

Photographs by Andrew Milligan (above) and Toby Melville (facing page)

It will be a moment of happiness and joy and light relief after some difficult times.

—BRITISH PRIME MINISTER DAVID CAMERON

ALL DECKED OUT: Nine days before the big event, Union Jacks festoon Regent Street, one of the West End's premier shopping venues. When British Prime Minister David Cameron declared the royal wedding a nationwide public holiday (on top of another public holiday the following Monday), many Londoners took advantage of the four-day weekend to leave town. But those who stayed—and the hundreds of thousands of tourists who joined them—reveled in London's festive atmosphere.

Photograph by Jonathan Hordle

WEDDING DAY

A Fairy Tale Comes True

The sky was overcast with a healthy chance of British rain. But then—just as the aubergine Rolls Royce Phantom carrying the bride glided up to the west entrance of Westminster Abbey—the sun broke through and gloriously shone down upon her. Everyone breathed a sigh of relief—from the tens of thousands in Trafalgar Square, to the hundreds of thousands in Hyde Park, to the millions glued to the telly at pubs and street parties throughout the realm, to the estimated two billion souls around the world who stopped whatever they were doing to watch Britain's future king marry his college sweetheart on live television. It would be fair weather for a spectacular event.

Inside the thousand-year-old abbey, midday light filtered down from the clerestory windows, bathing the nineteen hundred witnesses to the marriage in a cool, silvery blue light. The vivid elements of this timeless tableau included the black-and-white-checkered floor, the red-carpeted aisle, the queen's primrose yellow outfit with matching hat, and, at the altar, the bride's white silk gown and the groom's bright red Irish Guards uniform.

A few close family members and intimates sat in the screened-off choir section of the sanctuary, close to the altar, so for them the service seemed like an intimate affair. "It almost feels like a private wedding," remarked Lady Elizabeth Anson, first cousin to the queen. But the majority of honored guests, a veritable United Nations of royals,

DREAM CAKE: William and Catherine's extraordinary wedding cake took center stage at the queen's post-wedding reception for 650 guests at Buckingham Palace. Designer Fiona Cairns and her Leicestershire team glazed seventeen individual English fruitcakes with cream and white icing and decorated the entire confection with nine hundred individually iced flowers and leaves. The garland encircling the center of the cake matches architectural carvings in the palace's picture gallery where this photograph was taken. The companion champagne: Pol Roger NV Brut Reserve.

Photograph by John Stillwell

aristocrats, and celebrities, sat in the nave and watched the service on television monitors — just like the rest of us.

Overseeing the nearly flawless ceremony was the archbishop of Canterbury, Dr. Rowan Williams. His imposing aspect and sonorous voice were perfectly suited to the occasion. "Those whom God hath joined, let no man put asunder!" he intoned after William struggled to get the ring safely past Kate's second knuckle. In a pre-wedding interview, the archbishop shared his observation that William and Kate are "deeply unpretentious people," explaining that "they're responsible to the whole society; responsible to God for their relationship. And I think it's impressive that they've had that simplicity about it. They've known what matters, what's at the heart of all this."

In a steady cadence, Kate's younger brother, James Middleton, offered the lesson from Paul's letter to the Romans: "Let love be genuine," James read, "hate what is evil, hold fast to what is good; love one another with mutual affection; outdo one another in showing honor."

"This is a joyful day!" exclaimed the bishop of London, the Right Reverend Richard Chartres, in his address. "It is good that people in every continent are able to share in these celebrations because this is, as every wedding day should be, a day of hope." The bishop added a particularly piquant and inclusive note: "In a sense every wedding is a royal wedding," he said, "with the bride and groom as king and queen of creation, making a new life together so that life can flow through them into the future."

The music, all of it chosen by the royal couple, was British to its core — Edward Elgar, Vaughan Williams, Benjamin Britten, Hubert Parry — culminating in the gorgeous unaccompanied choral motet "Ubi Caritas," a recent work by Welsh composer Paul Mealor. Its yearning and spirited passages resolved themselves into a satisfying level of serenity. The composer, as it turns out, is a neighbor of the royal couple on the Isle of Anglesey in Wales.

With a brass fanfare and Catherine's deep curtsy to the queen, it was over. Wills and Kate were now the Duke and Duchess of Cambridge, walking together slowly down the aisle past a sea of big hats and gentlemen in morning dress, out into the dazzling white light of day, into an open carriage and a massive celebration of their marriage. The kingdom, it seemed, had a new lease on life. The crowd roared in Parliament Square and along Whitehall past the Cenotaph, through the Horse Guards, down the Mall, past the Victoria Monument, and into the forecourt of Buckingham Palace. In a sea of people, there was a woman in a red hat. She waved a poster-size photograph of William and Kate embracing. Neatly printed across the top was the message for the day: "Fairy tales do come true."

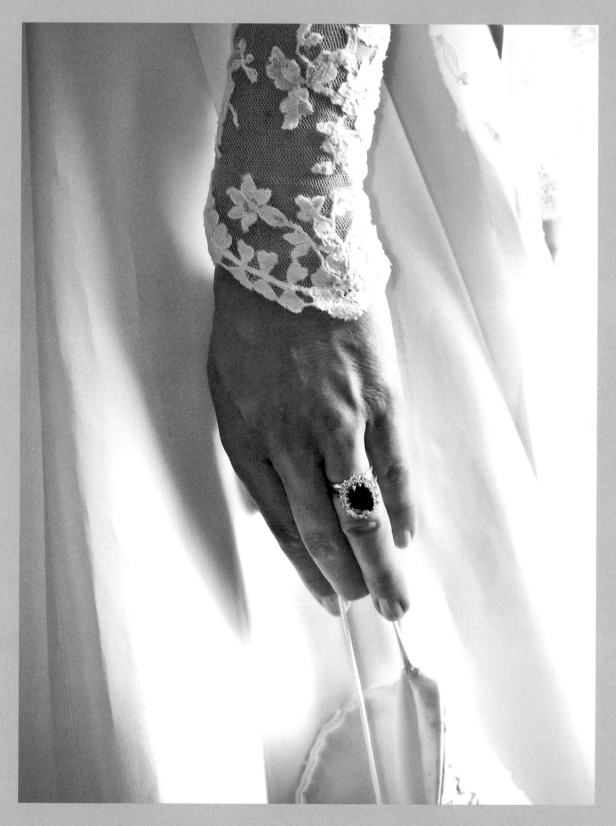

DETAILS: The bride's 18-carat sapphire and diamond engagement ring, originally worn by Princess Diana, perfectly complements the handmade French Chantilly and English Cluny lace sleeve on her Sarah Burton–designed wedding gown.   **Photograph by Ian West**

HAIL BRITTANIA: On Friday, April 29, good old British patriotism was on fervent display—along with a dollop of British cheek. Perhaps a million people flooded into London's streets, parks, and pubs to join the wedding festivities. Five thousand police were deployed; eight thousand video cameras monitored the streets; and security costs reached a reported thirty-two million dollars. Although fifty or so miscreants were arrested for various minor offenses, the massive crowd was, by most accounts, remarkably well behaved and generally very happy.

Photographs by Cordula Donhauser (facing page, top) and Carl Sims (facing page, bottom)

MAD HATTERS: Left, the Princesses Eugenie and Beatrice, twenty-one and twenty-three years old, respectively, arrive at Westminster Abbey. The daughters of Prince Andrew and Sarah Ferguson—or, more precisely, their hats—caused an immediate sensation. A Facebook group called "Princess Beatrice's ridiculous Royal Wedding hat" attracted more than 93,000 fans within a day of its debut. Superstar milliner Philip Treacy, who was responsible for the headpiece, also designed the slightly less sensational lids worn by Princess Eugenie, Victoria Beckham, and Camilla, Duchess of Cornwall. **Above**, Crown Prince Philippe of Belgium escorts Crown Princess Mathilde, who also sported a prodigious wedding-day chapeau.

Photographs by Ian Langsdon (left) and Tim Rooke (above)

ROYAL GUESTS: The nineteen hundred wedding attendees included friends and family of the couple, foreign royals, members of the British military, religious leaders, government figures, members of the diplomatic corps, leaders of the realms, and members of the royal household. **Above left**, Princess Anne, Prince Charles's younger sister, arrives at the Abbey. **Above right**, Prince Albert of Monaco and his longtime royal consort and fiancée, Charlene Wittstock, make their entrance. Their own royal wedding is only two months off.

Photographs by David Hartley (above, left) and Tim Rooke (above, right)

THE PRINCE AND THE PRIME MINISTER: Having forged a coalition government and imposed an austerity regime in Britain, forty-four-year-old Prime Minister David Cameron, **above left**, takes the morning off to attend the festivities. Prince Andrew, **above right**, a rear admiral in the Royal Navy, wears a formal dress uniform, as did his big brother, Prince Charles. Andrew's ex-wife, Sarah Ferguson, did not attend.

Photograph by Tim Rooke (above, right)

GET ME TO THE CHURCH ON TIME: Above, Princes Harry and William salute Whitehall's Cenotaph monument as they ride to Westminster Abbey in a Bentley limousine. The simple Portland stone slab, set in the middle of busy Whitehall Street, honors "The Glorious Dead" who perished in both world wars. **Left**, Michael Middleton and his eldest daughter ride from the stylish Goring Hotel to Westminster Abbey in a 1977 Rolls-Royce Phantom VI presented to Queen Elizabeth by the British motor industry on the occasion of her Silver Jubilee in 1978.

LAST MOMENTS OF BACHELORHOOD: Above, Westminster's dean, the Very Reverend John R. Hall welcomes Prince William and his best man, Prince Harry, to the hallowed thousand-year-old church. **Right**, escorted by Abbey's Receiver General, Stephen Lamport, the brothers enter the Abbey choir, the section of the sanctuary where the most intimate friends and family sit in close proximity to the wedding ritual.

Photographs by Tim Rooke (above) and Dominic Lipinski (right)

Now know ye that we have consented and do by these presents signify Our Consent to the contracting of matrimony between Our Most Dearly Beloved Grandson Prince William Arthur Philip Louis of Wales, K.G., and Our Trusty and Well-beloved Catherine.

—FROM QUEEN ELIZABETH II'S OFFICIAL INSTRUMENT OF CONSENT, REQUIRED BY THE ROYAL MARRIAGES ACT OF 1772

ROYAL YELLOW: The Very Reverend John Hall, thirty-eighth Dean of Westminster, welcomes Queen Elizabeth and the Duke of Edinburgh back to the Abbey, where the couple wed in 1947. Except for the bride and her father, the queen and her prince consort are, by tradition, the last to arrive before the service. The queen's sunny yellow outfit was widely praised in the fashion press as an attractive, optimistic choice. Dean Hall's yellow-gold cape came with the job.

Photograph by Ian Langsdon

GLOBAL CONGREGATION: Wedding guests stand to mark the arrival of Queen Elizabeth in Westminster Abbey. On the guest list: Queen Sophia of Spain, Queen Margrethe of Denmark, Crown Princess Victoria of Sweden, Princess Marie-Chantal of the Hellenes, Sir Elton John, David and Victoria Beckham, Guy Ritchie, Joss Stone, and Prince Harry's on-again, off-again companion, Chelsy Davy.

Photograph by Anthony Devlin

AUSPICIOUS SIGN: The sun broke through the clouds just as Kate Middleton arrived at Westminster Abbey, lending extra oomph to her ethereal veil. The bride's simple bouquet, designed by Shane Connolly, included lily of the valley (signifying purity of heart); hyacinth (constancy of love); a myrtle sprig, allegedly from a bush planted by Queen Victoria; and, of course, sweet william (another traditional signifier of constancy). In keeping with royal tradition, the Duchess of Cambridge returned her bouquet to Westminster Abbey after the service to be placed on the grave of the Unknown Warrior.

Photograph by Ian Langsdon

MAID OF HONOR: Above, Philippa Charlotte "Pippa" Middleton, twenty-seven, Kate's younger sister and her constant confidante throughout Kate's long courtship with Prince William. Pippa's simple, body-hugging ivory silk-crepe dress was designed by Sarah Burton at Alexander McQueen, who also designed Kate's wedding dress with its hand-embroidered tulle veil, lace sleeves and bodice, and nine-foot train. **Right**, Michael Middleton and his daughters enter Westminster Abbey.

Photographs by Tim Rooke (above) and Tom Pilston (right)

LONG WALK: To the strains of the hymn "I Was Glad" by Sir Charles Hubert Hastings Parry, and with all eyes upon them, Kate and her father, **above**, begin their long walk (more than five hundred feet) down the nave of Westminster Abbey. The hymn, composed for King Edward VII's coronation in 1902, was also sung at the wedding of Prince Charles and Lady Diana Spencer in 1981. **Right**, the bride, her bridesmaids, and her pages, led by the Dean of Westminster, John Hall, enter the choir.

Photograph by Adrian Dennis (above)

WAITING AT THE ALTAR: The future king, **left**, wears the distinctive red uniform of an Irish Guards mounted officer—including spurs. (Prince William, who is commissioned in all three military services, is an honorary colonel of the regiment.) Across his chest are the blue Garter Sash, the wings of the Royal Air Force, the Garter Star, and the Golden Jubilee Medal. **Above**, when Kate and her father finally joined him, William leaned in and apologized for all the fuss. "We were supposed to have just a small family affair," he quipped *sotto voce*.

Photographs by Dominic Lipinski

SCENES FROM A ROYAL WEDDING: Preceding pages, left: With the archbishop of Canterbury presiding, William wrestles his wedding band onto Kate's ring finger. The band was created by Welsh jewelers from a nugget of locally mined gold. In a nod to modernity, the groom chose not to wear a wedding ring, and the bride chose to promise to "love, comfort, honor, and keep" her husband rather than to "obey" him. **Preceding pages, right**: The newly married couple kneels in prayer.

Photographs by Dominic Lipinski (preceding pages, left) and Anthony Devlin (preceding pages, right)

MOSAIC LAW: As the wedding ceremony draws to a close, the London Chamber Orchestra strikes up "Crown Imperial," a march composed by William Walton and first performed in 1937 at the coronation of Prince William's great-grandfather, King George VI. With Prince Harry and Pippa Middleton in tow, the newlyweds take their leave. The spectacular medieval mosaic at their feet, known as the Cosmati Pavement, dates from the thirteenth century.

Photograph by Kirsty Wigglesworth

A NEW DAY: When the beaming newlyweds, **above**, emerged hand in hand from the West Door of the Abbey, a huge roar went up from the crowd. **Right**, a few moments later, Carole Middleton, Queen Elizabeth, and Camilla, Duchess of Cornwall, compare notes outside the Abbey as they await their carriages for the procession back to Buckingham Palace.

Photographs by Toby Melville (above) and Tim Rooke (facing page)

CARRIAGE TRADE: Following pages, **left**, new in-laws Prince Charles and Michael Middleton are about to share a carriage back to the palace with their wives, Camilla and Carole. Their carriage follows that of the queen and Prince Philip. **Following pages**, **right**, maid of honor Pippa Middleton and bridesmaid Margarita Armstrong-Jones ride to Buckingham Palace in an open landau. Margarita, age eight, is the late Princess Margaret's granddaughter.

Photographs by Tim Rooke (following pages, left) and Gareth Fuller (following pages, right)

We're quite a reserved lot, the British, but when we go for it, we really go for it.

—PRIME MINISTER DAVID CAMERON,
COMMENTING ON THE FESTIVITIES

A CONSTITUTIONAL MONARCHY: At a stately trot, Will and Kate's landau leaves Westminster, crossing Great George Street into Whitehall for the fifteen-minute ride to Buckingham Palace. Behind them is a resplendent Captain's Escort of the Household Cavalry—and the impressive spires of the Palace of Westminster, more popularly known as the Houses of Parliament. The day before the wedding, in a blog post called "God Save the Monarchy," influential political commentator and British expat Andrew Sullivan ruminated about the essential importance of the royal family to his native land: "When Britain is in crisis, or divided against itself, the monarchy does act as a unifier," he argued. "My rational modern mind cannot really defend it. But my emotional intelligence grasps the reason for its longevity. And hopes it survives forever."

Photograph by John Giles

Those people who were so recently sneering at her background ... will soon be lost in admiration of her poise and professionalism.

—ROYAL HISTORIAN
ANDREW ROBERTS

THE GREATEST SHOW ON EARTH: Walking down a five-hundred-foot aisle with the eyes of the world upon you. Check. Executing the entire service flawlessly. Check. Riding in an open coach past a million people, looking spectacular every inch of the way. Check. "It's obviously nerve-wracking," Kate once told television reporter Tom Bradby about the royal life, "because I don't know the ropes really." She could have fooled us.

Photograph by Gerry Penny

THE MONARCHY TODAY: Clockwise from above, Queen Elizabeth and her consort, Philip, Duke of Edinburgh; Prince William of Wales and his new bride, Catherine, Duchess of Cambridge; the groom's stepmother, Camilla, Duchess of Cornwall; and the mother of the bride and royal in-law, Carole Middleton, all ride in their respective carriages from Westminster Abbey to Buckingham Palace.

Photographs by David Hartley (facing page, bottom, left and right)

HAPPY AND GLORIOUS, LONG TO REIGN OVER US: The Metropolitan Police estimated that one million people hit the streets of London to catch a fleeting glimpse of the wedding parade. Street-party road closure applications for April 29 hit fifty-five hundred, indicating a kingdom-wide deluge of celebratory events. The Tesco retail chain reported selling 120 miles of bunting. And, from a population of sixty-two million, twenty-four million British television sets were tuned in to the ceremony. Amid the frenzy, the fiercely competitive *Daily Star* and *Daily Mirror* tabloids sported identical front pages on the wedding day: the headline "Happiest day of our lives," plastered over the same Mario Testino portrait of the smiling royal couple. At the end of the day, the Westminster Council deployed 130 road sweepers to clean up 140 tons of rubbish. Horse manure from the cavalry escorts was reportedly the biggest issue on an otherwise peaceful, proud, and, yes, happy day.

Photographs by Damien Meyer (left) and Kieran Doherty (above)

GRAND ENTRANCE: Inside the Buckingham Palace Quadrangle, the wedding procession pulls up to the venerable Grand Entrance. William and Kate, **above**, arrive first. Behind them are Prince Harry, Pippa Middleton, and the bridesmaids and pages. Minutes later, **right**, the queen and Prince Philip alight from their glass coach and head to the Throne Room, where photographer Hugo Burnand staged the official group portraits. After that, the queen hosted a grand midday reception for six hundred. Then the grandparents vacated the palace for a weekend at Windsor so that Prince Charles could host a roof-raising evening bash for three hundred of William and Kate's closest friends.

Photograph by Andrew Winning (right)

Any mother of an eight-year-old son chosen to be a page boy can be excused for having a touch of the butterflies before the big day arrives.

—TIGGY PETTIFER, PRINCE WILLIAM'S FORMER NANNY AND MOTHER OF PAGE TOM PETTIFER

HARRY AND PIPPA PLUS SIX: Best man Prince Harry and maid of honor Pippa Middleton expertly herd their flock of bridesmaids and pages out of the carriages, through the entrance hall, and into the Throne Room for the official wedding pictures.

Photograph by Andrew Winning

EYES OF THE WORLD: The world's press deployed a reported eighty-five hundred journalists, photojournalists, and technical staff to London to cover the royal wedding. Fourteen American television channels simultaneously broadcast live coverage, many of them with celebrity anchors—our Robert Jobson among them—bivouacked in a temporary, two-story studio with big glass windows, camouflaged with green paint and squeezed into Green Park for drop-dead views of the Queen Victoria Monument and Buckingham Palace.

Photograph by Geoffrey Robinson

PRELUDE TO A KISS: After the royal wedding party passed through the gold-tipped gates into the sanctity of Buckingham Palace, police estimate that a half-million spectators surged—for the most part, very politely—onto the broad pavements surrounding the Queen Victoria Monument, completely filling the huge plaza in front of Buckingham Palace. They were there to witness the first public kiss between their future king and queen.

Photograph by Oli Scarff

STOP-ACTION: It lasted only a moment, but photographer Peter Kneffel snapped three stop-action photos of the first kiss between the newlyweds. While he caught it, many in the crowd did not. They wanted a second kiss, and a few minutes later William and Catherine obliged.

Photographs by Peter Kneffel (right) and John Stillwell (facing page)

GRAND FINALE: On the **following pages**, the crowds and the royals alike enjoy the flypast over Buckingham Palace by the Battle of Britain Memorial Flight. The three World War II–era planes were an Avro Lancaster bomber, a Hawker Hurricane, and a Supermarine Spitfire. It was a fitting—and patriotic—finale to the public events on the royal wedding day.

Photograph by David Fisher (following pages)

DON'T WAIT UP: William, Kate, and Charles, **above**, leave Clarence House for the wedding-night revelry hosted by the Prince of Wales at Buckingham Palace. The party for three hundred guests stretched well past the official deadline of two in the morning.

Photograph by John Stillwell

OFFICIAL PORTRAIT: Left, the bride, groom, brides-maids, and pages in Buckingham Palace's Throne Room. **Clockwise from bottom left**, Eliza Lopes, the Duchess of Cornwall's three-year-old granddaughter; Grace van Cutsem, the groom's three-year-old goddaughter; Lady Louise Windsor, the queen's seven-year-old granddaughter; Tom Pettifer, the groom's eight-year-old godson; William Lowther-Pinkerton, ten-year-old son of the groom's private secretary; and The Honorable Margarita Armstrong-Jones, the queen's eight-year-old great-granddaughter. Hugo Burnand took Charles and Camilla's wedding portrait six years earlier (page 94), but the informality of this photo reflects the royal family's new face.

Photograph by Hugo Burnand

References

The quotations used in this book are taken from the sources listed below:

Page 6: "Royal wedding: 'Millions share in your joy,'" www.telegraph.co.uk, April 29, 2011.

9: "Princess Kate comments on royal wedding," Associated Press, April 29, 2011.

11: "Then came the event everyone was waiting for — the balcony kiss," www.independent.ie, April 30, 2011.

16: James Parton, Horace Greeley, et al., *Eminent Women of the Age: Being narratives of the lives and deeds of the most prominent women of the present generation* (S. M. Betts Co., 1868); "Victoria (r. 1837–1901)," www.royal.gov.uk.

21: Raegan Baker, "Biography: Princess Alice of Hesse and by Rhine," www.alexanderpalace.org; "Princess Alice Maud Mary," *Harper's Bazaar*, February 16, 1884; John Van der Kiste, *Queen Victoria's Children* (The History Press, 2004).

22: Carlo McCormick et al., *Trespass: A History of Uncommissioned Urban Art* (Taschen, 2010).

25: "Princess secluded on her honeymoon," *New York Times*, March 2, 1922.

27: "Abdication crisis," news.bbc.co.uk; "HM Queen Elizabeth, The Queen Mother, 1900–2002," www.winstonchurchill.org.

28: Tom Corby, "Obituary: Princess Alice, Duchess of Gloucester," www.guardian.co.uk, November 1, 2004.

30: James Collins et al., "Restoring the Windsors (and Windsor Castle too)," *Time*, December 1, 1997

36: Penny Junor, *The Firm: The Troubled Life of the House of Windsor* (Thomas Dunne Books, 2005).

38: Interview with the Princess of Wales, *Panorama*, broadcast in November 1995 on BBC1; transcript at www.bbc.co.uk.

43: Tina Brown, *The Diana Chronicles* (Broadway Books, 2007).

44: Andrew Morton, *Diana: Her True Story* (Simon & Schuster, 1992).

46: Christopher Andersen, *William and Kate: A Royal Love Story* (Gallery, 2010).

49: Ibid.

53: "Harry: Camilla isn't the wicked stepmother," *Daily Mail*, September 15, 2005.

54: Andersen, *William and Kate*.

59: Caroline Davies, "Prince William: Give my father a break," *Daily Telegraph*, June 21, 2003.

63: Brown, *The Diana Chronicles*.

68: Andersen, *William and Kate*.

77: Interview with Prince William and Miss Catherine Middleton, broadcast November 16, 2010, on ITV; transcript at www.princeofwales.gov.uk.

78: "Royal wedding: profile of Kate Middleton," *Daily Telegraph*, February 23, 2011.

85: Andersen, *William and Kate*.

90: Widely reported but unattributed to a source.

95: Katie Nicholl, *William and Harry: Behind the Palace Walls* (Weinstein Books, 2010).

101: Robert Jobson, *William's Princess: The Love Story That Will Change the Royal Family Forever* (John Blake, 2006).

104: Ibid.

105: Andersen, *William and Kate*.

108: Rebecca English, "Kate runs the paparazzi gauntlet on her 25th birthday," *Daily Mail*, January 10, 2007.

114: "Prince William splits from Kate," news.bbc.co.uk, April 14, 2007; Christopher Wilson, "A historic act of folly and supreme egotism on the part of the Prince," *Daily Mail*, April 15, 2007.

116: Laura Collins and Louise Hannah, "As Kate re-emerges more tanned and confident, a new Middleton girl takes a bow," *Daily Mail*, May 27, 2007.

117: Emma Cowing, "The other Middleton girl," www.living.scotsman.com, November 4, 2008; Victoria Moore and Rebecca English, "The Sizzle Sisters: Kate and Pippa are one of the hottest double-acts in town," *Daily Mail*, June 19, 2007.

119: Simon Perry, "Prince William and Prince Harry announce Concert for Diana," *People*, December 12, 2006.

120: Claudia Joseph, *Kate Middleton: Princess in Waiting* (William Morrow Paperbacks, 2010).

131: "Princes join charity bike rally," news.bbc.co.uk, October 18, 2008.

136: "Prince William to join RAF Search and Rescue," www.princeofwales.gov.uk, September 14, 2008.

Tired but happy, and ready for the future, Wills and Kate leave Buckingham Palace by helicopter on the day after the wedding. **Photograph by John Stillwell**

142: The Royal Society, "About us," www. royalsociety.org/about-us/; "Prince William becomes a Royal Fellow of the Royal Society," www.princeofwales.gov.uk, June 22, 2010.

147: Faye Schlesinger, "Meet the in-laws! Kate Middleton is given a foretaste of that wry royal sense of humour," *Daily Mail*, November 16, 2010; video at www. itnsource.com, November 16, 2010; "Royal wedding: Prince William to marry Kate Middleton," news.bbc.co.uk, November 16, 2010.

148: "An interview with Prince William and Miss Catherine Middleton" (video and transcript), www.princeofwales.gov.uk, November 16, 2010.

149: "Untold stories behind Kate's 18-carat sapphire," www.today.com, November 16, 2010; "An interview with Prince William and Miss Catherine Middleton" (video and transcript), www.princeofwales.gov.uk, November 16, 2010.

152: Ibid.

153: Ibid.

154: Ibid.

157: "Royal engagement 'delights' Kate Middleton's parents," AFP (Agence France-Presse), November 16, 2010; Schlesinger, "Meet the in-laws!"

158: "Prince Harry on William's engagement: 'I get a sister!,'" www.usmagazine.com, November 16, 2010; "They have been practising long enough: Charles and Camilla welcome 'wicked' news of engagement," *Daily Mail*, November 16, 2010; "Video: Royal wedding: Prince Charles 'thrilled' by engagement, www.telegraph.co.uk, November 16, 2010.

160: Autumn Brewington, "Official wedding souvenirs for sale," voices.washingtonpost. com, December 21, 2010.

166: Katie Couric, "UK's Cameron: A joyful moment amid difficult times," www. cbsnews.com, April 27, 2011.

183: Jessica Derschowitz, "Queen Elizabeth II gives royal wedding her formal consent," www.cbsnews.com, April 21, 2011.

193: "Royal wedding coverage," *Today*, broadcast April 29, 2011, on NBC.

202: "Royal wedding quotes: some of the best lines of the day," www.telegraph. co.uk, April 29, 2011; Andrew Sullivan, "God save the monarchy," www.thedailybeast.com, April 28, 2011.

205: "Royal wedding quotes."

213: Rhodri Owen, "Royal wedding: Shân Legge-Bourke on page's preparations," www.bbc.co.uk, April 26, 2011.

The following books are among those used as sources:

HRH Princess Alice, Duchess of Gloucester, *Memories of Ninety Years* (Collins-Brown Ltd., 1991).

Andersen, Christopher. *William and Kate: A Royal Love Story* (Gallery, 2010).

Battiscombe, Georgina. *Queen Alexandra* (Trans-Atlantic Publications, 1984).

Brand, Emily. *Royal Weddings* (Random House, 2011).

Brown, Tina. *The Diana Chronicles* (Broadway Books, 2007).

Jobson, Robert. *William's Princess: The Love Story That Will Change the Royal Family Forever* (John Blake, 2006).

Joseph, Claudia. *Kate: The Making of a Princess* (William Morrow Paperbacks, 2011).

Joseph, Claudia. *Kate Middleton: Princess in Waiting* (William Morrow Paperbacks, 2010).

Junor, Penny. *The Firm: The Troubled Life of the House of Windsor* (Thomas Dunne Books, 2005).

Morton, Andrew. *Diana: Her True Story* (Simon & Schuster, 1992).

Nicholl, Katie. *William and Harry: Behind the Palace Walls* (Weinstein Books, 2010).

Parton, James, Horace Greeley, et al., *Eminent Women of the Age: Being narratives of the lives and deeds of the most prominent women of the present generation* (S. M. Betts Co., 1868).

Pope-Hennessy, James. *Queen Mary, 1867–1953* (George Allen and Unwin Ltd., 1959).

Van der Kiste, John. *Queen Victoria's Children* (The History Press, 2004).

The following websites are among those used as sources:

www.africa2008.blogspot.com
www.alexanderpalace.org
www.armedforces.co.uk
www.bbc.co.uk
www.cbsnews.com
www.ceros.com
www.cnn.com
www.dailymail.co.uk
www.flickr.com
www.flightglobal.com
www.fordham.edu/halsall/
www.gamefair.co.uk
www.guardian.co.uk
www.harpersbazaar.victorian-ebooks.com
www.hellomagazine.com
www.heraldicsculptor.com
www.history.com
www.horseandhound.co.uk
www.hubpages.com
www.independent.ie
www.inquirer.net
www.itnsource.com
www.mirror.co.uk
www.news.aol.ca
www.news.bbc.co.uk
www.nowmagazine.com
www.nytimes.com
www.officialroyalwedding2011.org
www.people.com
www.princeofwales.gov.uk
www.royal.gov.uk
www.royalsociety.org
www.scotsman.com
www.telegraph.co.uk
www.thedailybeast.com
www.thenma.org.uk
www.thepeerage.com
www.thestar.com
www.time.com
www.today.com
www.usatoday.com
www.usmagazine.com
www.vanityfair.com
www.victorianlondon.org
voices.washingtonpost.com
www.wikipedia.org
www.winstonchurchill.org

Off to a new life in dad's vintage Aston Martin DB6 Volante

Contributors

Created by David Elliot Cohen

Text by David Elliot Cohen and Curt Sanburn

Foreword by Robert Jobson

Designed by Peter Truskier and David Elliot Cohen

Page production and image processing by Peter Truskier, Premedia Systems, Inc.

Copyedited by Sherri Schultz

Proofread by Sharon Vonasch

Production assistance by Lucas Cohen

Thanks To:

Tory Brown

Michael Fragnito, Barbara Berger, Caroline Mann, Elizabeth Mihaltse,
    Fred Pagan, and Gillian Berman of Sterling Publishing

Humfrey Hunter of Hunter Profiles

James G. Kauffman, Jr.

Angela and Grace Seeger

Photo Sources

AFP/Getty Images: 71 (bottom), 75, 96, 97, 107, 140, 150–151, 152, 159

Alpha/Landov: 93 (right), 114, 116 (right), 117 (left), 121, 134, 172

BEI/Rex USA: 8, 41 (2), 42, 45, 46, 47, 79 (2), 89, 95, 103, 104 (right), 111, 112, 117 (right), 120, 126, 127, 145, 153, 160, 167, 173 (bottom), 175, 176 (2), 177 (2), 179, 180, 188, 191, 199, 200, 207 (3), 210, 214, 218–219

Clarence House Press Office: 146, 155 (both photos © 2010 Mario Testino)

Daily Mail/Rex USA: 49

EPA/Corbis: 76

EPA/Landov: 12, 161, 173 (top), 174, 178, 182, 186, 192, 193, 204, 216, 217

Everett Collection/Rex USA: 29, 33

Fox Photos/Getty Images: 34

Getty Images: 23, 35, 39, 40, 48, 50, 51, 52, 54, 56, 57, 58, 60, 61, 62, 64, 66, 67, 69, 71 (top), 72, 73, 84, 85, 86, 87, 88, 91, 92, 93 (left), 94, 99, 102, 104 (left), 106, 110, 115 (bottom), 118, 119, 128, 129, 131, 132–133, 137, 141, 142–143, 156, 162 (2), 195, 220, 221, 222

Hulton Archive/Getty Images: 20, 24

Hulton-Deutsch Collection/Corbis: 26

Indigo/Getty Images: 100, 123, 135, 138, 139, 144, 224

Middleton Family/British Monarchy: 80, 81

Ministry of Defense/Anwar Hussein Collection/Getty: 105

PA Photos/Landov: 1, 4–5, 7, 101, 108, 109, 116 (left), 122, 154 (2), 164, 181, 185, 189, 194, 197, 201, 203, 206

Popperfoto/Getty Images: 16, 19, 31, 37

Princess Diana Archive/Getty Images: 55

Reuters/Corbis: 113, 115 (top)

Reuters/Landov: 163, 165, 168, 171, 190, 198, 208, 209, 211, 212, 215

Splash News/Newscom: 82 (bottom)

Time-Life Pictures/Getty Images: 63, 65, 68, 70

Topical Press Agency/Getty Images: 25, 32

UK Press/Getty Images: 74

Whitehotpix/Newscom: 82 (top), 83

Wireimage/Getty: 98, 124, 125, 130

Xinhua/Landov: 10